THE
NEW YORK TIMES
Natural Foods
DIETING BOOK

THE
NEW YORK TIMES
Natural Foods
DIETING BOOK

YVONNE YOUNG TARR

Illustrations by the author

Weathervane Books • New York

*I dedicate this book to
Aldora, Carlene, Joan, Kathy,
Laura Lee, Louise and Nanette.
With a special thanks
to my son for the sun.*

Text design by Anita Duncan

contents

v

introduction

This book is about a new way to live your life . . . that is, as a slim, trim, more energetic and healthier human being. Merely being slim, it's true, is not enough to make you have a more rewarding life, and being in the best of health is not enough to make you your most attractive self. But being slim and attractive, full of pep and a new-found vitality, may open the way to a happier, perhaps even a longer, life.

That makes good sense, doesn't it? We both know that overweight is an unsightly, uncomfortable, unhealthy and unnatural phenomenon! The question is, what's to be done about it? What magic formula is going to turn you into the slender, vigorous person you have always wanted to be? What indeed?

If you are reading this, it is reasonable to suppose that you need or would like to lose weight. It is equally reasonable to suppose that your interest in natural foods has been aroused. The question you are probably asking right now is, "Why diet with natural foods as opposed to any other?"

The answer is threefold. One, because when you are properly nourished it's easier to reduce quickly and comfortably. Two, because natural foods catapult you into a new vitality. And three, because by encouraging a proper diet, natural foods make it possible for you to *stay* slim once you have reduced.

If you are conscientious and don't cheat, even for a minute, this diet will trim pounds of unattractive, unwanted weight from your hips, waist, upper arms, thighs, back, stomach

1

. . . everywhere! Unlike the typical weight-loss diet, which deprives you of the vitamins and minerals you need to maintain a healthy, vigorous body, the Natural Foods Weight-Off Regimen provides you with all of the vital nutrients so essential to good health. For perhaps the first time in your life, you will be eating foods that contain a maximum of proper nutritional values with an absolute minimum of unnatural and unhealthy food additives. And all the while, you will be losing weight safely and effectively, without the excessive hunger pangs and loss of health and energy that almost invariably accompany unhealthy fad diets.

The health aspect of dieting is tremendously important. Eminent authorities have presented overwhelming evidence that the average American diet is woefully inadequate. It is high in fats, lazy starches, sugars and poisonous additives. The hard-working B vitamins are polished from our rice, removed from our breads and ransacked from our sugars. Our meats are laced with antibiotics. Our poultry is shot through with hormones. Our fruits and vegetables are saturated with deadly pesticides. Our processed foods are devitaminized, demineralized and abound in artificial preservatives and coloring matter. Add to this the nutritional deprivations of the ordinary reducing diet, and it is not hard to see why your health may suffer grievously.

The Natural Foods Weight-Off Regimen attempts to right all of these nutritional wrongs, and it attempts to do so in a logical, sensible manner! For example, without a bit of sweet in the morning your blood-sugar level will not rise sufficiently, and early morning pep loss is the result. Without a daily supply of iron, vitamin B and adequate proteins high in amino acids, your body is deprived of elements essential to good health. The Natural Foods Weight-Off Regimen recommends an egg, honey and whole grain bread for breakfast. Result? Enough energy and nourishment to start your day off right and get you through to lunch without gnawing hunger pangs. Lunch is high in proteins, vitamins and minerals, as is the well-balanced dinner. There's even a delicious and healthful yoghurt, honey and fruit snack and an herb tea break to strengthen you whenever your resolve begins to falter.

This diet utilizes only nourishing and easily digested honey or raw sugar, instead of sterile and devitalized white sugar. Few Americans realize that granulated sugar, molasses, even maple and corn syrups are so altered in processing that they

2

are actually artificial sweeteners. In the opinion of some experts, they are also habit-forming and should really be classified as drugs. Sugar provides a quick lift, a sense of exhilaration which quickly fades and produces a craving for more and more white sugar in the form of cakes, candies and sweet carbonated drinks . . . a diet- and health-damaging vicious circle. Honey, on the other hand, is a natural sugar, does not have to be transformed by the body, and therefore is not only *not* habit-forming, but actually causes your cravings for sweets to be quickly satiated.

In short, the Natural Foods Weight-Off Regimen is the one diet that supplies your body with the vitamins, minerals and other body essentials you need to sustain life and good health, pep and energy. It eliminates the poison-harboring foods that endanger your health and well-being. It frees you from the "eat sugar, want sugar" syndrome. This is, in fact, the one weight-loss diet that actually starts you on the road to a more vigorous, more healthful life while you lose pounds and pounds of unwanted overweight . . . the one diet that helps you to become the trim, slim, healthier, more vigorous person you've always dreamed you could be!

the natural foods weight-off regimen

•

At last, a great new way to diet. . . . A great new way to lose unwanted, unattractive overweight without damaging your health, without suffering excessive hunger pangs, without becoming nervous, cross and irritable! A great new way to nourish your body, improve your general health and well-being, and become a more vital, more alive person while you lose weight!

Does it seem to you you've heard that song before? If you have, forget it! In fact, forget everything you've heard or learned about diets before today. Forget the "hard-boiled egg diet." Forget the "grapefruit diet," the "water diet," the "doctor's diet," the "nurse's diet," the "former-fatties diet," and all the rest. Diets come and diets go, but one sad fact remains. If any of those diets worked half as well as their inventors claimed, every adult in America, including you, would be a slim, svelte 102 pounds, and nobody would be reading these pages right now!

Why? The truth is that all those fad diets demand the impossible. Unless you have the strength and the will power of a Hercules, the patience of a saint, and a well-developed streak of masochism besides, you simply can't live with hunger pangs and deprivation indefinitely. It's not only demoralizing, it's injurious to your health.

In this scientific day and age, I'm sure you accept the fact that overweight is unhealthy, but are you aware that those outlandish fad diets can be equally deleterious to your health? They rob your body of proper nutrition, your skin of its glow,

5

your hair of its luster, your life of its sense of well-being. You long for a normal meal. You crave sweets and starches. You never really feel satisfied.

If diets are trying and as difficult and as ineffectual as I claim, then what prompts me to add another to the list? Simply the fact that the Natural Foods Weight-Off Regimen is different! It not only helps you to lose weight safely and easily, but it nourishes you properly besides! You eat nutritious whole grains, health-promoting honey, natural foods rich in minerals and high in vitamin content, and perhaps most important, you no longer ingest poisonous preservatives, food additives, artificial coloring matter and other potentially injurious chemicals. And all the while, your excess pounds melt away! You feel more vital, more alive and infinitely more comfortable, because almost miraculously your unnatural cravings for sweets and starches disappear, and losing weight becomes easier and pleasanter than you ever thought possible! I know because it happened to me!

I used to be a sugar-maniac! Sweets and white bread were my mainstay. White toast with jam, cookies, sandwiches, sweet tea, rich French desserts . . . Little wonder that every few months I had to go on some reducing diet or other to shake off those unwanted pounds. Then, having accomplished my mission, it was back once again to my super-sweet, super-starchy daily diet.

You see, as a sugar-maniac, not to mention white-bread fiend, I often felt tired and irritable. I lacked pep and energy. Then, in the course of doing research for a new book, I came across several fascinating books on vitamins and body chemistry,* and a new world opened up to me. I discovered why I ate so poorly. Why, try as I would to change my eating habits, I just couldn't break my addiction to sugar. These volumes, written by authorities, pointed out that all starch is turned to sugar by the body. This meant, in effect, I was eating sugar . . . with sugar. I simply wasn't getting the proper nourishment. Oh,

---

* Frances Moore Loppé, *Diet For a Small Planet,* New York: Ballantine, 1971. Paperback original.

Adelle Davis, *Let's Eat Right To Keep Fit,* New York: Harcourt Brace Jovanovich, Inc., 1970, revised from 1954 edition. Paperback edition available from New American Library, New York.

Bodog Beck and Doree Smedley, *Honey and Your Health,* New York: Bantam, 1971. Paperback reprint of 1944 revised edition.

my meals were large and costly enough, but they were essentially devoid of the vitamins and minerals I needed to sustain good health. My body was malfunctioning much like an engine trying to run on sugar syrup instead of fuel.

These authoritative books went on to explain that white sugar, corn and even maple syrups are so altered during the course of processing that they should actually be considered artificial sweeteners.

We tend to think of them as harmless or even useful foods, but actually these artificial sugars are stimulants powerful enough to produce a shock effect on our digestive systems, which in turn causes our vital organs to work furiously. This "lift" is followed quickly by a slump, a "down" that causes us to crave another white sugar "pickup" . . . another piece of candy, another piece of cake and so on. White starches cause much the same reaction since they are changed into sugar by our bodies. It seemed hard to believe that my fatigue was actually the result of improper diet, but the more I read, the higher the evidence mounted and the more obvious it became that it was time for a change. And why not? What harm could it do to eat more healthfully? I decided to take the plunge.

What a drastic change! One day I was eating nothing but white starches and sugars, rich sauces and white rice. The next day I was practically paranoid about a slice of white bread or a teaspoon of white sugar! I wouldn't even look at white rice and I was stirring honey into my tea with the knowing smile of a witch with a secret potion!

That's how the natural-foods bug bites! Once you become aware of the harm you have been doing to your one and only body—the body that must last you (hopefully) to a ripe old age—you are appalled at the thought of ingesting anything that might harm it!

I came to believe, and I believe even more fervently now, that vitamins and minerals are the saviors of the body, and that preservatives, chemical sprays and vitamin-deficient processed foods are the agents of its downfall. I refuse to eat poisons or take into my body anything that is not beneficial in some way. Calories do count, unfortunately, and unhealthy foods contain at least as many of them as healthy ones do! A food must pay its way in nutrition if it's going to add to my intake of calories or carbohydrates. It's the only way I know of to stay slim and healthy at the same time!

When I became a natural foods addict, my health did

7

improve emphatically! Gradually, I became less tired, less ir-ritable, and I discovered to my great joy that I could eat foods that I hadn't dared to go near for years! But of course, what things in this life are without drawbacks? Munching fruits and nuts and salads (not to mention eating dates and honey and yoghurt and brown rice and bulghour and barley and adzuki beans and sunflower seeds) with careless abandon had its penalties, and before I knew it, I had gained 15 pounds in a matter of months. I started to plump up in a few of the wrong places. I wanted to be healthy . . . yes, but not fat and healthy! No matter how it is acquired, even if your cholesterol intake is low, overweight is simply not good for you. And that's defeating the purpose of natural foods eating, isn't it? So, back to the old calorie and carbohydrate charts I went, only this time I was determined to lose weight without losing all of the wonderful benefits of the natural foods I had come to love so well. There must be a way, I decided, and there was! All it took was careful planning. So, carefully plan I did, and this book is the result. . . . Low calorie recipes and snacks, low carbohydrate recipes all carefully tested, all tasty enough to satisfy the author of gourmet cookbooks (me).

But the best was yet to come. As I tested and tasted and wrote, I tried one diet plan after another. Utilizing my new-found knowledge, I placed myself on diets that were high in nutrition requirements, until I happened upon the best diet of all. It provides the quick lift of honey to raise your blood sugar in the morning and start your day off energetically.

It utilizes whole grains and breads to provide the B vita-mins so vital to health. Eggs are included to supply vitamins A and B and amino acids. Health-promoting yoghurt is an integral part of the overall plan—plus the use of delicious, fully tested, vitamin-rich natural food recipes so good no one (especially you) will know you're dieting. I followed this plan and my weight slipped down from 120 to 110 to 105. One morning my scale registered at 103 and I quickly began to overeat to be sure I wouldn't lose any more weight. Enough was enough! I wanted to be slim, but I didn't want to disappear completely.

The best feature of the diet, as far as I was concerned, was the fact that I never felt hungry. I simply never suffered from the hunger pangs I had experienced on other diets. Friends who have tested the Natural Foods Weight-Off Regimen also report quick and steady weight losses without excessive hunger pangs. You'll find the basic plans on the following pages. Why not check them out and begin your diet tomorrow? You have only good health to gain and weight to lose. But before you begin, if you have any doubts about whether or not you should diet, please consult your physician.

The Natural Foods Weight-Off Regimen is a liberal diet. It doesn't make impossible demands of you. It takes into account the fact that you didn't get heavy overnight, and therefore it doesn't attempt to slim you down overnight. Rather it encourages you to lose safely and surely, it gives you a choice of techniques by which this may be accomplished, and all are within the framework of a healthy, sensible natural foods regimen.

Essentially there are three basic methods which you may use interchangeably. Method number one is called . . .

The Substitution Method
—For Persons Who Need Only Lose
a Few Pounds

In this method, whenever practical to do so, you substitute low calorie foods for the high calorie dishes that are making you overweight. Let us assume, for example, that every night before you retire, you are accustomed to having a rich snack . . . perhaps a wedge of chocolate cake, a dish of ice cream, or something equally fattening. You are tucking away anywhere from 300 to 900 calories over and above what you actually need to sustain yourself.

Now suppose that, instead of that calorie-rich chocolate cake (or whatever) that you have every evening, you substitute instead a relatively low calorie snack. For example, Walnut Snack, page 234, is only 73 calories, delicious, and a lot better for you. By substituting that low calorie dish for your accustomed snack, you have saved yourself several hundred heavy calories. That, in essence, is what substitution is all about.

To carry it a step further, let us assume that during the

9

course of the day you repeat that operation several times. Perhaps you substitute a few low calorie nibbles for those two slices of bread at lunch, a low calorie vegetable for those high calorie potatoes, or a low calorie dessert for that gooey French pastry you might otherwise have. With relatively little effort you have saved yourself a great many more unnecessary calories. You feel none the worse for your efforts, and most important, by the week's end you may have saved a total of thousands of calories. You will actually be losing weight at a slow, steady rate. Surely that is a step in the right direction!

The Low Calorie Method

—for Maximum Weight Loss

Low calorie dieting is, of course, the basis for virtually all diets. During the normal course of each day you are accustomed to ingesting a certain amount of food, each item of which has a specific caloric content. When the amount of calories you take into your body exceeds the amount you use up in the form of energy, you have created a surplus which is stored in various portions of your anatomy in the form of fatty tissue. The classic technique for losing weight, then, is to consume less . . . to take into your body fewer calories than your body needs to live on, thereby forcing your body to burn off that stored-up fat in the form of energy.

Following is my low calorie diet. Note that while you are allowed a wide selection for lunch and dinner, breakfast remains constant, and with good reason. The objective is to produce a high blood-sugar level to get you off to a peppy start in the morning and to keep you that way until lunchtime. This is achieved by use of a protein (egg) in conjunction with natural sugars (honey), and it is an important feature of this diet.

Low Calorie Diet

1	egg, boiled, fried or scrambled without butter	75
1	slice whole wheat bread with butter	110
2	teaspoons honey (one may be used in your tea or coffee)	44
	tea or coffee without sugar, milk or cream	0
	Total	229

Lunch   *Calories*

Any low calorie vegetable, fish or cheese recipe in
this book that does not exceed   225
or
½ cup cottage cheese topped with
   ¼ cup yoghurt and
   ½ apple, chopped or sliced, and
   2 teaspoons honey
tea or coffee without sugar, milk or cream   0
                                     Total   225

Dinner   *Calories*

Any low calorie meat, fish or vegetable recipe in
this book that doesn't exceed   175
or
½ large slice calf's liver dipped
   in 1 tablespoon wheat germ and fried
   in 1 teaspoon butter

Any low calorie grain recipe in this book that
doesn't exceed   190
or
you may combine your 175 calorie meat, fish or
vegetable recipe and your 190 calorie grain recipe

and have *one* meat, fish or vegetable *and* grain recipe that doesn't exceed 365 calories

Any salad recipe in this book that doesn't exceed   40
or
1   green pepper and
1   cup steamed broccoli
     with sea salt

                                        Total   405

Dessert or Late-Night Snack   *Calories*

Any dessert or snack recipe in this book that doesn't exceed   185
or
¾ cup plain yoghurt (no more) and
½ apple, chopped or sliced, with
1   tablespoon honey

                                        Total   185

                              Total for day   1044

Low Calorie Maintenance

If you have followed your diet (or diets) conscientiously, have not cheated more than once or twice, have neither lied to yourself nor miscounted your calories or carbohydrates accidentally on purpose, you should be nearing your desired weight. Now it's time to think about ending your stringent dieting and beginning your maintenance program.

This is the period of adjustment when you begin to eat a bit more lavishly by increasing your caloric intake to 1150 calories per day for one week. During this interval, weigh yourself every morning to make sure you are not gaining. Even one pound of extra weight at this crucial time indicates a need to return to your calorie count of the previous week. Your body must get used to your new weight; this it will do, but slowly. Don't be in too much of a rush to eat more or you will undo what you have accomplished. And don't forget your vitamin supplements. You will want to continue them throughout your life.

You will find, to your pleasure, that the Natural Foods Weight-Off Regimen has brought your body to a healthier peak than it has probably ever reached before. Due to your intake of proper nutrients and your abstinence from white flour and sugars, you should no longer crave unhealthy sweets. For this same reason you should have no desire to return to your former habit of overeating. A daily count of 1250 calories (for men a little more) should allow you to eat healthfully, to feel satisfied, and to remain thin, beautiful and healthy for the rest of your life.

The Low Carbohydrate Method

—for Rapid Weight Loss

A method that has become increasingly popular in recent years is known as the low carbohydrate diet. In this method, as the name implies, you strictly curtail the amount of carbohydrates you eat daily. You eat, instead, foods in which the carbohydrate content is very low or nonexistent. Meat, for example, is rich in proteins and contains virtually no carbohydrates. Fish, poultry, fats, butter, most cheeses and eggs are equally low in that fattening substance, and these are the foods that form the basis for your diet . . . for without carbohydrates you cannot gain weight!

This does not mean to say that you may eliminate carbohydrates completely. On the contrary. Your body does require some carbohydrates, but not in excessive amounts. The average person attempting to lose weight should have no more than 58 grams of carbohydrate daily, and in this diet you should neither exceed nor go below that amount.

The low carbohydrate diet, which follows, has been carefully planned around that magic number. The advantages of the diet are fairly obvious. You may eat substantial quantities of low carbohydrate foods while you are reducing, which is the reason many people prefer this method to the low calorie regimen. Ideally one should remain on the low calorie diet until weight loss starts to taper off and then switch to the low carbohydrate diet. Switching back and forth alleviates boredom and provides for maximum weight loss.

Low Carbohydrate Diet

Breakfast   *Carbohydrates*

1 egg, boiled, fried or scrambled with butter .... tr *
1 slice whole wheat bread with butter 12
1 teaspoon honey (this may be used in your tea or coffee) 6
tea or coffee without sugar but with heavy cream (not milk) if you desire 0

Total 18

Lunch

Any low carbohydrate soup, fish or cheese recipe in this book that doesn't exceed 10
tea or coffee with or without heavy cream 0

Total 10

Dinner

Any low carbohydrate meat, fish or egg recipe in this book that doesn't exceed 10
Any low carbohydrate vegetable or salad recipe in this book that doesn't exceed 10

Total 20

Dessert or Late-Night Snack

Any low carbohydrate dessert or snack recipe in this book that doesn't exceed 10
herb tea without sugar or cream 0

Total 10

Total for day 58

* tr = trace

Low Carbohydrate Maintenance

I personally find the low calorie maintenance habit more comfortable than the low carbohydrate maintenance plan. Some people, however, respond more favorably to the low carbohydrate schedule. If you are one of these and wish to base your lifetime eating habits around this method, it is important to "spend" your increased carbohydrate count on whole grains, fresh vegetables and some raw fruit.

When you reach your desired weight, increase your carbohydrate intake to 70 per day. Weigh yourself every morning and carefully note whether your weight is beginning to slip upward. If so, immediately go back to 58 grams of carbohydrate daily. A week later, try once again. Repeat this procedure until your weight no longer rises and you have boosted your carbohydrate intake to 75–80 per day.

Continue your vitamin supplements and your Natural Foods Regimen. There is no better way to enjoy good health, a slim, attractive body and perhaps even a longer life.

natural foods...
what's going on
here, anyway?

Why this sudden, frenzied advance by the wealthy and the not so, the youthful and the once-were, toward the local health foods store? Why this impassioned pilgrimage to the farmer who "doesn't spray"? Why are the French food fanatics (myself included) nibbling on dried fruits and nuts with only an occasional venture into haute cuisine? Repeat question: What is going on here, anyway?

Answer: We citizens of the USA are fed up with being fed poorly. We are tired of feeling sick and sick of feeling tired. We are rebelling against being tricked into eating preservatives so that the manufacturer and the grocer can keep boxes on the shelf for longer periods of time. We are rebelling against hormone-filled poultry which may have deleterious long-range effects on our health. We are dead set against lovely DDT-sprayed apples—tasteless and more deadly than the ones the witch slipped Snow White. In other words, we are becoming a nation of indignant but determined health freaks.

If you do not see yourself as the health-foods-fanatic type and are slightly embarrassed when purchasing yoghurt and brown rice and alfalfa tea, relax. You're having a very natural reaction. I couldn't see myself in that role either. I *adore* French food . . . and Italian food . . . and Moroccan . . . and Japanese . . . and Javanese . . . and Chinese . . . and American. I thrive on Mousse de Saumon en Gelée and Boeuf Bourguignon and such, but you never can tell, can you, what pollution that poor fish has been sipping during its unnatural lifetime, or what nasty chemicals that prize cow has been in-gesting. Or, for that matter, what those nostalgic old World War II planes have been spraying on your peaches. Unfortu-nately, it's either off to the health foods store or grow your own.

Do you wince when you realize our country's bounty is no longer pure, that the grasshoppers are dying in those amber waves of grain, and the birds are no longer singing among the fruited plains? Act out your concern by purchasing a small, gnarled (but really tasty), unsprayed apple! Don't fret; it's one small step, but it's an important one. If everyone did the same, the grocers couldn't sell that big, beautiful, poison-filled piece of fruit, and soon the spraying would stop and the birds would be singing again. Think about it as you sit in your kitchen and munch your unsulfured, honey-dipped, dried apple slices and feel healthy.

food additives... an ugly and unhealthy business

Filthy air, polluted water, excessive noise . . . these are realistic and ever-increasing menaces to our way of life, but they are only part of the story . . . only part of the problem that you and I and our fellow humans face. According to a great number of our most enlightened scientists, air, noise and water pollution are not nearly as hazardous to our health and well-being as is the pollution of the foods we eat. That, in their estimation, is the number one danger we face.

I don't want to sound like an alarmist. I am not anxious to be mistaken for a fanatic, and the reality is that I am not. I believe in reason and moderation. Unfortunately the food industry—the one industry upon which you and I depend in great measure for survival—does not. In this mad technological maelstrom in which we are trapped, you and I and our loved ones are being slowly, surely and inexorably poisoned. And that, believe it or not, is a *conservative* statement.

This isn't the time or the place to become involved in a delineation of the 3000 or more chemical additives contained in the foods you eat every day. This is not a highly technical book. It does not purport to be one. It *is* a well-researched and tested diet cookbook, but I do feel there are certain facts of which you should be apprised. Read them and believe them. Unhappily, they are quite true.

I mentioned in the previous paragraph that the food-processing industry, as of this moment, is using upward of 3000 chemical additives of various types and toxicities annually. Fewer than half of them have been subjected to anything even vaguely resembling exhaustive laboratory testing. Our breads, cakes, meats, poultry and vegetables are contaminated with chemicals of every type and description, and no experts anywhere, the Food and Drug Administration included, can tell us for sure whether those chemical additives are safe or not. They can hazard educated guesses, they can speculate, but they cannot tell us with certainty whether or not a great many diseases—from cancer through mental retardation—may be caused by chronic poisoning resulting from those chemical additives which you and your family consume day after day, year after year, in ever-increasing quantities.

Food additives are a $500,000,000 a year industry. Close to a billion pounds of additives are consumed during the course of a single year, and that quantity is increasing by leaps and bounds!

Now a manufacturer can make fruit juice without fruit, meat products without meat, birch beer without birch, and root beer without roots! He can take a handful of soybean protein that costs pennies, shape it and flavor it and color it until it resembles anything he likes—from fruit to nuts. The soybean hamburger you feed your dog looks more like red meat than meat does. The bacon bits you throw into your salad look and taste just like bacon, but they're not! They are merely soybeans and chemicals.

Whether you are aware of it or not, there is a revolution in food-processing going on right now, and you are smack in the middle of it, financing it with your dollars and paying for it with your health! Take sodium nitrite and sodium nitrate, as a case in point. These chemicals are recognized to be potent human poisons and laboratory carcinogens as well. They are used to fix the color of meat so that the hot dogs and cold cuts you eat remain a bright pink instead of turning a dull, natural brown. They are also used to preserve smoked fish, tuna, salmon, etc. When sodium nitrates reach your stomach, they combine with your body acids to form a chemical that is a potent cancer-producing agent.

As another example, consider the two most widely used preservatives in the food-processing arsenal . . . BHT and BHA. Great Britain forbids their use in all foods intended for babies and children, but American kids have them every day in their dry cereals, with every slice of packaged bread they eat, and in innumerable other packaged foods as well. Laboratory rats that eat BHT show up with enlarged livers and skin tumors. But rats aren't children, and since the evidence against BHT isn't overwhelmingly conclusive, it, like BHA, remains a mainstay of the food-processing industry.

Chemical food colorings have probably been the biggest villains of all. There are few packaged foods that don't contain them in some small quantity. Notwithstanding the fact that many colorings have been proved to produce cancer in the laboratory and have been disapproved for use, numerous others, which the FDA's own technicians have found cause ulcers and tumors in rats, remain.

Who is going to protect you from these potentially dangerous chemicals? Not the understaffed, overworked, industry-harassed Food and Drug Administration. The only one who is going to give you the protection you should have is yourself! You have to stop eating hot dogs. You have to stop eating cold cuts. You have to stop eating smoked fish and hundreds of other chemical-loaded, processed foods. That way, and only that way, you will stop poisoning yourself. Get back to fresh, natural foods. Foods naturally dried, ground or canned. Remember, it isn't wise to fool around with Mother Nature.

natural foods...
how to find them

What does "natural" mean as applied to foods? How does a food become "organic"? Tremendous amounts of newspaper and magazine space have been devoted to the new popularity of organic foods, but most people have only a hazy idea of what that term actually means. There are several important steps that must be followed before a food appears in your health foods store proudly bearing the "natural organic" label.

To begin with, of course, all organic foods must spring from soil that is entirely devoid of man-made chemicals. That means no artificial fertilizers, no pesticides, no laboratory-produced agricultural aids in any shape or form whatsoever!

Organic crops are fertilized solely by organic means. Leaves, humus, composted natural fertilizers and rock minerals are used to treat and enrich the soil. While the plants are growing, no chemical sprays, toxic or otherwise, are used.

Insect pests as well are controlled by natural methods . . . that is, by the use of ladybugs, praying mantises, purple martins, and other natural enemies of the marauders.

Only fruits, vegetables and grains grown by these methods are deemed to be truly organic. All others are impostors.

The second step in the natural food chain concerns the production of meat and poultry. Here, too, the rules are equally stringent. Cattle and poultry which are to bear the organic label must be fed only organically grown fodder. They may not be injected with or fed antibiotics or hormones or other stimulants to growth. Indeed, they must be prepared for market

23

without the use of chemicals of any type for any purpose whatsoever.

Processing, too, or perhaps I should say especially, must deviate from the procedures generally prevalent in the food industry. All freezing, drying, packaging or canning must be consummated without recourse to synthetics or additives of any type. No chemical preservatives may be used. No fillers, no artificial flavoring or coloring matter may adulterate any food, animal or vegetable, which is to be sold as organic. The object is not to produce a food so shot through with preservatives that it will last indefinitely on the grocer's shelf, or so doctored with artificial coloring as to be inordinately attractive, but rather to produce simple, healthful, chemical-free food that is tasty, nutritious, and devoid of possibly harmful, long-range effects on the consumer's health and well-being.

In addition to the manner in which it has been grown and the care and concern with which it has been processed, a food must retain its vital nutrients in order to be considered "organic" or "natural." A flour which came from organically grown grain would lose that designation if, in the course of processing, all of the healthful elements had been removed. White flour is a perfect example of this. Devitaminized, demineralized, "fortified" with artificial vitamins and preservatives, it could by no stretch of the imagination be considered organic. The same applies to white sugar, cottonseed products, corn syrup, hydrogenated fats and all other foodstuffs which are the end results of the chemist's skills and the food processor's machinations.

Organic foods, then, require highly specialized treatment from the time they are planted to the time they reach your kitchen. This explains their relative scarcity and consequently their higher cost. Fortunately, however, the situation is changing rapidly.

I thoroughly believe that by the time you read this book, a natural foods store will have popped up like a bean sprout right at your elbow. At the moment, there is a health foods outlet born about every thirty seconds, or so it seems. After years of deprivation, the natural foods enthusiast is being confronted at every turn with a "Mother Nature's Garden" or a "Natural Nutrition Center" or some such. Natural foods have become big business and that means increased availability . . . a welcome change.

You probably have a health foods store in your town

already (if your town happens to be New York City or Los Angeles or Chicago or any other major metropolitan area, you will have no trouble finding them). For one reason or another your town may not have been blessed with one yet. If you're in this sad predicament, on page 260 is a list of natural foods concerns that will send foods by mail. Or, on second thought, why not start a store of your own?

If the following recipes call for ingredients unfamiliar to you (such as alfalfa sprouts, dulse, etc.), refer to the Glossary on page 263 for definitions.

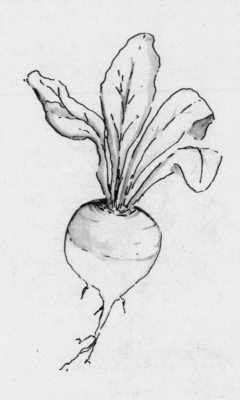

tips

- Buy fresh fruits and vegetables only in small amounts that can be speedily consumed.
- Eat fresh fruits and vegetables as soon as possible after purchasing. Vitamin and mineral counts go down during storage.
- Steam vegetables or cook them in a tiny amount of water over medium or low heat.
- Always drink or use the water from cooking vegetables.
- Never peel organically grown fruits or vegetables if their peels are edible. Many vitamins and minerals are contained in the skin.
- Rinse rather than wash or scrub organically grown produce. Vitamins and minerals are lost with excess washing.
- Refrigerate fruits and vegetables as soon as possible. Nutrients are lost when the produce is allowed to remain for any length of time in a warm temperature after gathering.
- Cook food with a cover, whenever possible, so that vitamins and minerals do not disappear into the air with the steam.
- Always cook in enamel, glass or ceramic utensils, *never* in aluminum. Aluminum flakes off and enters your body with the food you eat.
- Cook meat as little as possible because protein is injured by prolonged high heat.
- Store herbs at room temperature in airtight containers. Open only when necessary and close containers as quickly as possible.

- When you have a choice, buy products in glass jars. Avoid metal or plastic containers.
- Skim off excess fat during cooking of meats, soups or stews.
- Take small bites and chew each bite thoroughly. This not only aids your digestion but helps cut down the amount of food you actually consume.
- If you *must* nibble, eat sunflower seeds and raisins *one at a time*. Yes, it's possible—but not easy. Don't forget to keep track of every calorie or gram of carbohydrate.
- One-fourth teaspoon of honey will completely dissipate sugar craving.
- Chew on a piece of cinnamon stick for a no-calorie snack.
- Avoid all white sugar and white flour. These are often death to a diet. They produce a violent reaction in the system and cause sugar-mania, an unnatural craving for sweets.
- When you're following a low carbohydrate diet, never snack with fruits. They are tremendously high in carbohydrates. Follow your carbohydrate snack list. (See page 241.)

basic
natural foods
and recipes

Yoghurt

What is a more perfect food than yoghurt? This snowy-white cultured milk with the texture of silk is delicious, nutritious, adaptable and inexpensive. No wonder it has been a food staple for over 4000 years! From biblical times to the present, yoghurt has nourished the old and the young, the fat and the thin, the rich and the poor. From unpretentious European housewife to master of haute cuisine, all have known and appreciated its subtle taste and health-giving goodness.

Yoghurt is of special interest to me not merely because of its more obvious attributes, but also because of a little-known medical property it happens to possess. I am one of those unhappy individuals who has an unpleasant reaction to antibiotics. I am not allergic in the usual way, but on those occasions when I am forced to take them, I suffer from an unpleasant side effect. My tongue turns a painful and unlovely lead-gray. Honestly. If it has never happened to you, don't scoff. Just consider yourself extremely lucky. If this particular phenomenon is in the realm of your experience and you have not been introduced to yoghurt by your physician, as I was by mine, allow me the pleasure . . . "Antibiotic sufferer, please meet yoghurt." "Yoghurt, please meet antibiotic sufferer." Result: a corrected digestive tract. How does yoghurt work such miracles? Very simply. Every cubic centimeter of yoghurt contains some 200,000,000 or so of the helpful bacteria known as *Lactobacillus bulgaricus*. When antibiotics are taken to kill off the harmful bacteria in your system, many of the good bacteria in the digestive tract also fall victim, and your digestion suffers. Several glasses of yoghurt, however, and your bacterial garden is replanted and ready to go to work. Once again, you are on your way to a sweet stomach and a pink and healthy tongue.

I hope that this discussion of yoghurt and good health hasn't made you think of it as a medicine. True, yoghurt is easier to digest than milk. It is beneficial to ulcer victims and it does replenish helpful bacteria, but its primary value remains as a smooth, piquant and nutritious food, and as such it has been consumed for centuries in a dazzling variety of dishes, both peasant and gourmet. It is equally delicious with meats, grains, vegetables and fruits, and *is as low in calories as it is high in nutrition!* How many other foods can make that claim?

Homemade Yoghurt

1 pint

Make your own delicious yoghurt at home. It's so easy and so economical, you need never be without a creamy bowlful in your refrigerator.

		Calories	Carbohydrates
¼	cup commercial yoghurt	30	3
1	pint milk	320	24
	Total	350	27

Allow commercial yoghurt to reach room temperature. Heat milk in a glass pot to wrist temperature. Stir the yoghurt into the milk.
Wrap the glass pot in a warm towel. If your oven has a pilot light, place yoghurt there and allow it to remain undisturbed overnight.
If not, set the pot in the sun or pour it into a thermos bottle and see that it remains quiet for at least 8 hours.
Refrigerate yoghurt when it is tangy and thick.
Always save a few tablespoons for future batches.

31

Yoghurt Dressing

Equally delicious served with cold vegetables, cold fish or as a salad dressing.

		Calories	Carbohydrates
½	cup yoghurt	60	6½
1	egg yolk	60	tr
¼	teaspoon dry mustard	0	0
¼	teaspoon sea salt	0	0
½	teaspoon organic raw sugar	8½	½
1	teaspoon lemon juice	1	tr
	Total	129½	7
	Total for 1 tablespoon	9	½

Beat all ingredients together.
Refrigerate.
Serve cold.

Yoghurt Mayonnaise

		Calories	Carbohydrates
2	tablespoons butter	200	tr
4	tablespoons whole wheat flour	268	28
1	cup milk	160	12
1	cup yoghurt	120	13
1	egg yolk	60	tr
	juice from ½ lemon	10	3
1	tablespoon raw organic sugar	51	3
¾	teaspoon dry mustard	0	0
½	teaspoon salt	0	0
	Total	869	59
	Total for 1 tablespoon	19	1

Melt butter in skillet and stir in flour. Add milk all at one time and stir over medium heat until the sauce is thick and smooth. Remove from heat and beat in the egg yolk, lemon juice, sugar, mustard and salt. Stir in the yoghurt and cool. Refrigerate.

Homemade Cottage Cheese

If you feel ambitious, try making your own cottage cheese. Save the whey. It is marvelous for baking.

	Calories	Carbohydrates
1 pint sour milk	320	24
sea salt to taste	0	0
Total	320	24
Total for 1 tablespoon (with whey discarded)	16	tr

Heat sour milk to wrist temperature in a glass pot.
Hold a triple thickness of cheesecloth over a glass bowl. Strain the heated sour milk, reserving the whey (or liquid) for baking. The curds remaining in the cheesecloth are the cottage cheese. Salt lightly.
Mix with 1 tablespoon of cream if the cheese is used in carbohydrate recipes.
Chill.

Whole Wheat Bread

Makes 3 loaves—16 slices each

Only one bread recipe is necessary if it is the *right* one. This is the best of hundreds I've tested.

Bread baking is good for the soul as well as the arm muscles and not nearly as tricky as you may think. Why not try it one day when it's raining and you plan to stay indoors anyway? The smell of baking bread, not to mention the satisfaction of that first delicious bite, is more than worth the effort.

		Calories	Carbohydrates
3	cups water	0	0
2½	tablespoons baker's yeast	33	5
¾	cup honey	792	204
¼	cup safflower oil	500	0
7½	cups unsifted, stone-ground whole wheat flour	515	110
¾	teaspoon sea salt	0	0
5	tablespoons dried, defatted coconut flakes	46	15
5	tablespoons sunflower seed kernels	105	5
	Total	1991	339
	Total for 1 slice	42	7

Allow all ingredients to come to room temperature. Combine water, yeast and honey in a large mixing bowl. Allow to stand for 5 minutes. Add oil, 5 cups flour and salt, and beat for 100 strokes or for 8 minutes at low speed in your electric mixer. Do not shirk on this process or your bread will not be light and crunchy.

Stir in the remaining 2½ cups flour or enough to make a stiff dough. Sprinkle coconut, sunflower seeds and 2 tablespoons flour on a bread board or pastry cloth. Turn dough onto this and knead 100 times, using more flour if necessary to keep the dough from sticking.

This is the best exercise I can think of to firm the upper arms and pectoral muscles, so go at it energetically.

Oil a large bowl and place the dough in it, smooth side down. Turn the dough greased side up, cover and place in an unlit oven, or in some other place that is warm and free from drafts. Let rise 1 hour or until double in bulk.

When double in size, punch the dough down to its original size, cover and let rise as before. Knead to original size, divide into 3 equal parts, and shape into 3 loaves.

Place in 3 loaf pans generously greased with butter. Cover and let rise once again in the unlit oven until the dough reaches to tops of the pans. (It will continue to rise during baking.)

Bake in an oven preheated to 350°F. for 50 minutes or until golden brown on top.

Brush lightly with butter and cool on wire racks.

Freeze if desired.

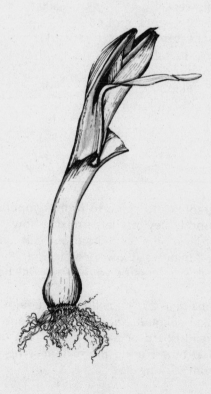

Chicken Stock

Yield: 6 cups

		Calories	Carbohydrates
1	small chicken	—	0
1	veal knuckle	0	0
3	quarts water	0	0
4	chicken feet	—	0
3	stalks celery with leaves	15	6
1	clove garlic, whole	0	0
1	bay leaf	0	0
⅛	teaspoon thyme	0	0
	Total	15	6
	Total for 1 cup	2½	1

Place chicken, veal knuckle and water in a large soup kettle.
Clean and skin the chicken feet (or ask your butcher to do it
for you) and add to the kettle.
Bring slowly to a low, rolling boil and cook for 1 hour, skim-
ming scum from the surface when necessary.
Wash the celery and cut into 2-inch pieces. Add the celery,
garlic, bay leaf and thyme, and simmer for 2 hours.
Strain the stock, cool and then chill it. (Reserve the cooked
chicken meat for other uses.)
Remove fat and store the stock in the refrigerator or freeze.

Vegetable Stock

Yield: 6 cups

Save parsley, watercress and mushroom stems, those slightly wilted outer leaves of cabbage and lettuce, slightly soft tomatoes, onion skins and celery leaves, even apple skins. They all enhance this rich vegetable stock.

		Calories	Carbohydrates
1	tablespoon butter	100	tr
3	small onions	90	30
2	carrots	40	10
5	celery stalks with leaves	25	30
1	small bunch parsley	3	0
3	tomatoes	75	0
5	medium-sized mushrooms	40	5
5	scallions	18	4
	any vegetables you have been saving in your stock jar (if you haven't saved any, double the amounts of onions, carrots and celery mentioned above)	125	70
3	quarts water	0	0
	Total*	516	149
	Total for 1 cup*	86	25

Melt the butter in a pan.
Wash and slice the vegetables and stir them into the butter in the pan.
Bake them in a moderate oven for 30 minutes.
Add the water and simmer on top of the stove for 4 hours.
Strain the stock, place in jars and refrigerate.
Remove the butter that rises to the top. Freeze in ice-cube trays if desired.
Refrigerated stock will keep for 5–7 days, frozen stock for 2–3 weeks.

* The calorie count of stock is lower than the total of its parts because much of the butter and vegetable fiber is strained off.

Beef Stock

Yield: 6 cups

Freeze your meat bones and save your uncooked vegetable scraps in a jar to make the best bouillon you've ever tasted.

		Calories	Carbohydrates
2	pounds beef or veal bones (or both)	—	—
	any scraps of meat you have on hand	—	—
1	pound piece lean beef*	—	—
1	roast chicken carcass (optional)	—	—
2	small onions	60	10
1	carrot	20	5
3	celery stalks with leaves	15	6
	any vegetables you have been saving in your stock jar (if you haven't saved any, double the vegetables mentioned above)	55	16
3	quarts water	0	0
	Total	150	37
	Total for 1 cup	25	6

Have the bones cut into small pieces. Wash and slice vegetables. Spread the bones and meat in a roasting pan and cover with vegetables. Bake at 350°F for 50 minutes. Discard the fat, add water, simmer on top of the stove for 4 hours, skimming off any scum that might rise.
Strain the stock, place in jars and refrigerate.
Remove the fat that rises to the top. Freeze in ice-cube trays, if desired.
Refrigerated stock will keep for 5 days, frozen stock for 2–3 weeks.

* The beef count is not included because only the broth is used. The beef may be served as a main course or sliced cold for lunch.

How To Grow Sprouts

Sprout-growing is super-easy and fascinating to observe. Even if sprouts were not nutritious and crunchily delicious I'd advise you to grow some just for the fun of it. Almost any seed or bean can be sprouted. Best of all are probably delicate alfalfa, sweet winter wheat and spicy mustard seed sprouts. Sesame seed, lentil, soy and mung bean sprouts are equally tasty. It is important that the seeds or beans be *whole* and *raw* or they will not sprout. Harvest when sprouts are a little over 1-inch tall.

Directions

Method I: Buy an inexpensive plastic sprouter and follow directions included in the package.

Method II: My interest in sprout-growing began nearly 10 years ago when my preoccupation with Chinese cooking was at its peak. Since commercial sprouters were not readily available at that time, I experimented until I discovered the following foolproof method. Dampen thin, sponge dishcloths and place them on a cookie sheet. Arrange mung beans (or others) in the waffle-like depressions. The beans or seeds may be close together but should not be one on top of the other. Cover the pan *loosely* with waxed paper and place in an *unlit* oven. Every day sprinkle with a tiny bit of water. Re-cover with waxed paper and replace in unlit oven. In a few days your sprouts will be ready to harvest.

Basic Bulghour Recipe

Makes approximately 50 tablespoons

(If you are a vegetarian you can omit bacon and substitute vegetable stock for chicken stock.)

		Calories	Carbohydrates
1	small onion	30	8
1	slice bacon	47	½
1	tablespoon butter	100	tr
1	cup bulghour	500	132
⅛	teaspoon sea salt	0	0
	a pinch each of nutmeg and		
	rosemary	0	0
2½	cups basic chicken stock	5	2
	Total	682	142½
	Total for 1 tablespoon	14	3

Mince onion and bacon.
Sauté onion, bacon, bulghour, salt, nutmeg and rosemary in butter until onion and bulghour are golden.
Add chicken stock and bring to a boil.
Lower heat and simmer for 15 minutes or until bulghour is tender.
Serve hot, or refrigerate and use in other recipes.

Vigor Cereal

		Calories	Carbohydrates
¼	cup wheat germ	61	8
½	cup rolled oats	75	13
2	tablespoons rice polish	39	6
¼	cup flaked wheat	200	46
¼	cup flaked rye	180	40
6	dates	30	8
¼	cup raisins	70	19
¼	cup sesame seeds	140	5
¼	cup sunflower seed kernels	86	3
¼	cup whole almonds	176	3
1	tablespoon soy powder	27	2
¼	cup coconut meal	38	12
	Total	1122	165
	Total for 1 tablespoon	22	3

Place the wheat germ, rolled oats, rice polish, flaked wheat, and flaked rye in a glass baking dish. Bake for 10 minutes in an oven preheated to 250°F.

Heap this mixture and the dates on a chopping board and use a large knife to reduce to a coarse powder.

Stir in the remaining ingredients.

Store in a mason jar.

Homemade Bean Curd

I think perhaps it's wise to include a recipe for bean curd since it cannot be dried and boxed, and most health food stores do not carry it. The best place to buy bean curd is in a Chinese grocery store. If your town does not have one and you wish to sample this uniquely flavored, spongy delicacy, I suggest you try this easy recipe.

		Calories	Carbohydrates
1	cup full fat soy flour	250	38
¾	cup cold water	0	0
2	cups boiling water	0	0
1	large lemon	4	1
	Total	254	39

Mix the soy flour with the cold water. Beat until the paste is smooth. Add the boiling water, stir, then boil for 5 minutes over medium heat. Stir in the strained juice from the lemon and let the mixture cool. When it has coagulated, drain through cheesecloth until no more water drips off. Cut into square pieces and store in brine. Change the brine every 2 days. Use as indicated in this and other cookbooks.

Sushi

Serves 2

Sushi is an unusual Japanese dish featuring cold rice. The rice is cooked and while hot is flavored with a syrup made with vinegar and sugar. After cooling, the rice is formed into cubes or balls and served with a wide variety of garnishes. This recipe, featuring brown rice, is unusually tasty.

		Calories	Carbohydrates
¾	cup cooked brown rice	525	68
2	tablespoons vinegar	4	2
2	tablespoons organic raw sugar	100	10
	Total	629	80
	Total for 1	315	40

Heat rice. Boil vinegar and sugar until syrupy.
Mix rice and hot syrup and cool.
Form into cubes or balls and serve cold with garnishes.

The following garnishes are good when served with Sushi:
    Chicken and cheese balls
    Mushrooms stuffed with bulghour and almonds
    Mushrooms with cashew stuffing
    Marinated mushrooms
    Sweet and salty skewered veal
    Crabmeat omelet
    Scallops and shrimp en brochette
    Crunchy chicken balls
    Broiled sweet potato
    Eggplant with miso
    Zucchini-stuffed summer squash
    Fried acorn squash
    Raw cucumber stuffed with crabmeat
    Asparagus with sesame seeds

Fruit and Nut Wheat Bars

Makes 20 bars

This recipe makes a great snack to take with you when you are travelling.

		Calories	Carbohydrates
2	tablespoons butter	200	tr
5	tablespoons organic raw sugar	255	15
1	large egg	75	tr
½	cup whole wheat flour	200	42
¼	cup wheat germ	61	8½
¼	teaspoon baking powder	0	0
½	teaspoon cinnamon	0	0
¼	cup finely chopped, raw cashew nuts	200	4
¼	cup pitted, chopped, dried prunes	140	16
¼	cup chopped, dried apricots	39	10
2	tablespoons honey	132	34
	Total	1302	129½
	Total for 1	65	6

Cream butter and sugar until smooth. Beat in egg. Combine wheat flour, wheat germ, baking powder and cinnamon, and beat this into the egg mixture, a spoonful at a time. Press this wheat flour paste between two sheets of plastic wrap until flat and thin and rectangular in shape.
Refrigerate for 1 hour.
Chop the nuts, prunes and apricots, and mix them with honey. Quickly peel the plastic wrap from the wheat flour paste and place it on a greased cookie sheet. Spread with the honey–nut mixture and bake for 15 minutes in an oven preheated to 350°F.
Cool slightly and cut into bars.

Honey

Eons ago, when man was still a nomad, when he caught his food on the hoof or plucked it from wild trees of the forests, centuries before he began to cultivate the fertile valleys or domesticate animals for food, honey was a prized treat for his primitive palate. Honey is one of the oldest and most revered foods the world has ever known. Considered a sacred substance and a symbol of purity, honey was entombed with the ancient Egyptian kings to sip on their trip to eternity. The Moors considered honey an aphrodisiac (probably because of its ability to produce quick energy), and the early Greek philosophers were convinced honey promoted long life. Greek athletes traditionally banished fatigue by gulping a mixture of honey and water after their participation in the strenuous Olympic games. Honey has nourished us through all the centuries, but today, when we most need its health-giving qualities to enrich our devitalized diets, we turn our backs on it and use instead that dead substance, white sugar.

It's true, every grain of white sugar we consume is so altered from its natural state that it must be considered an artificial sweetener . . . a highly concentrated, addicting, powerful stimulant that produces a shock effect upon the nervous system as well as the vital organs. Unfortunately, maple and corn syrups heated to high, nutrition-destroying temperatures are therefore also devitalized and worthless, even potentially dangerous, sweeteners by the time they reach your grocer's shelf.

Not so—delicious, pure, health-promoting honey. Honeybees, unlike human manufacturers, carefully store the flower nectars they gather in tiny, airtight, wax capsules, thereby preserving honey's natural sugars (dextrose and levulose), its digestion-aiding enzymes, as well as its many minerals and vitamins. Since honey need not be oxidized by the digestive system, it does not cause a craving for more and does, in fact, quickly satiate a desire for sweets.

46

Contrary to common belief, honey is not always the sweet, golden-colored liquid found in jars in supermarkets.

There are over 250 kinds of honey produced by bees collecting nectar from at least 1800 flowers, plants and trees *in the United States alone*. These range from the dark brown, mineral-rich buckwheat honeys of Michigan, Ohio, and New York State through the tart fireweed honeys of Oregon and Washington . . . from the fragrant orange-blossom honey of California to the pale-amber clover honeys so familiar to us all. Delicious also are the exotic and aromatic honeys of foreign lands: Scottish heather honey with its lavender tint, pale-green gooseberry honey from France, pure white Siberian honey, fragrant acacia honey from Hungary, not to mention African, Australian, Brazilian, Persian, Indian and Mexican varieties.

Whether liquid, granulated, or comb honey . . . from the farm next door or far-off Siberia . . . whether snow white or the black Brazilian variety, do treat yourself to this delectable natural treat.

appetizers

Low Calorie Appetizers

Chicken and Cheese Balls

Makes 10 small balls

		Calories
¼	cup chopped, cooked chicken breast	185
1	1-inch cube cheese, grated	70
2	teaspoons grated onion	2
⅛	teaspoon curry powder	0
⅛	teaspoon sea salt	0
1	tablespoon wheat germ	15
10	watercress leaves	0
	Total	272
	Total for 1	27

Pound the chicken and cheese together in a mortar.
Add the onion, curry powder and sea salt.
Mix well, form into 10 small balls and roll in wheat germ.
Spear each watercress leaf and chicken ball with a wooden pick.
Chill.
Serve cold.

Eggplant Appetizer

		Calories
¼	medium-sized eggplant	11
1	small onion	30
1	slice bacon	47
1	stalk celery	5
1	tablespoon buckwheat honey	66
1	tablespoon ketchup	15
½	teaspoon lemon juice	1
⅛	teaspoon cinnamon	0
⅛	teaspoon sea salt	0
	a pinch each of cloves and marjoram	0
	Total	175
	Total for 1 portion	87

Peel eggplant and cut into ½-inch squares. Parboil for 3 minutes and drain well.

Chop onion, bacon and celery, and fry over medium flame for 5 minutes.

Add remaining ingredients and cook, stirring constantly for 2 minutes more.

Serve cold or at room temperature.

Bulghour Dip

Serves 5

		Calories
2	tablespoons basic bulghour recipe (see page 41)	26
1	tablespoon ketchup	15
	several pinches of cayenne pepper	0
5	whole wheat crackers, 2-inch square each	138
	Total	179
	Total for 1	36

Prepare basic bulghour recipe or use cold, leftover basic bulghour.
Mix bulghour, ketchup and cayenne pepper.
Chill.
Serve on crackers.

Tomato and Raisin Stuffed Onions

		Calories
1	large onion	50
1	teaspoon butter	33
1	small tomato	24
½	teaspoon organic raw sugar	8
1	teaspoon raisins	11
	a pinch each of nutmeg and sea salt	0
1	teaspoon wheat germ	5
	Total	131

Scoop out the center of the onion. Reserve center. Place the whole onion in boiling salted water and cook for 5 minutes. Remove and drain.

Meanwhile, sauté the scooped-out center in butter until it is transparent.

Chop the tomato and add it, along with the raisins and spices, to the onion.

Cook over low heat until the tomato mixture is fairly thick, then stir in the wheat germ.

Fill reserved onion with tomato mixture.

Bake for 20 minutes in an oven preheated to 350°F.

Sprout-Filled Avocado

Serve this filling first course whenever you plan a simple meat or fish and salad meal. It is also marvelous "as is" in place of lunch.

		Calories
½	avocado	185
½	small tomato	24
1	scallion with 3 inches green top	4
½	hard-cooked egg	37
2	tablespoons alfalfa sprouts	0
2	teaspoons yoghurt mayonnaise (see page 33)	12
	Total	262

Peel avocado half and remove seed.
Chop tomato, onion, egg and 1 tablespoon of sprouts.
Stir in enough yoghurt mayonnaise to barely moisten. Fill the avocado with this mixture and top with the remaining 1 tablespoon of sprouts.
Chill for 2 hours.
Serve cold.

Guacamole

Serves 2

Here's a spicy dip from south of the border. It's also superb served on a lettuce leaf as a luncheon salad.

		Calories
½	avocado, peeled and seeded	185
½	small onion	15
½	tomato	18
½	clove garlic, peeled and crushed	0
½	teaspoon lemon juice	0
⅛	teaspoon sea salt	0
¼	teaspoon chili powder	0
1	tablespoon yoghurt (optional)	8
	Total	226
	Total for 1 portion	113

Finely chop avocado, onion and tomato. Mix all remaining ingredients.
Chill.
Do not prepare more than 1 hour in advance of serving or avocado may darken.

Mushrooms Stuffed
with Bulghour and Almonds

This is a delicious hors d'oeuvre or snack served hot or cold; the recipe doubles, triples or quadruples beautifully.

		Calories
5	fairly large mushrooms	50
2	teaspoons butter	66
1	scallion with 3 inches green top	4
1	tablespoon chopped almonds	53
1	tablespoon basic bulghour recipe (see page 41)	13
1½	tablespoons ketchup	23
½–1	cup milk	100
	Total after discarding milk	309
	Total for 1 mushroom	62

Wash mushrooms and remove the stems. Set the mushroom caps to drain on paper towels.

Melt the butter in a Teflon skillet, mince the mushroom stems and the scallions, and sauté them in the melted butter for 5 minutes, stirring frequently. Stir in the chopped almonds, bulghour and ketchup. Use this almond mixture to stuff the mushroom caps.

Pour the milk into a flat, ovenproof dish until it reaches the level of about ½ inch. Place the caps in the milk and bake for 30 minutes in an oven preheated to 350°F. Carefully remove the stuffed mushrooms and place them on a plate. Discard the remaining milk.

Serve hot or cold.

Eggplant Pickles

70 pieces

		Calories
½	eggplant	22
	sea salt	0
1	teaspoon dry mustard	0
1	tablespoon soy sauce	10
1	tablespoon organic raw sugar	51
1½	tablespoons vinegar	3
	Total	86
	Total for 1 piece	1

Cut ½ eggplant in half lengthwise.
Cut into ¼-inch slices. Arrange pieces on plate and sprinkle with sea salt.
Allow to stand for 15 minutes.
Make a paste of the mustard, soy sauce, sugar and vinegar.
Squeeze eggplant between paper towels to remove liquid.
Place eggplant pieces in a quart jar with a lid. Pour in vinegar mixture, tighten lid and gently rotate jar until all pieces are soaked with the paste.
Refrigerate for at least 3 hours.
Gently rotate the jar from time to time.
Serve cold.

Oriental Almonds

Guests love these!

		Calories
½	cup almonds	425
1	teaspoon butter	33
⅛	teaspoon Chinese five-spice (or a pinch each powdered anise, cloves, ginger and nutmeg)	0
⅛	teaspoon sea salt	0
1	tablespoon tamari (soy sauce)	10
	Total	468
	Total for each nut	12

Toast the almonds in butter over very low heat.
Sprinkle with the spices and tamari and stir until the nuts are dry.

Low Carbohydrate Appetizers

Fish–Dill Pâté

Makes 2 portions

A subtle and thoroughly gourmet first course or luncheon dish is Fish–Dill Pâté. Serve it if you must entertain while you're counting carbohydrates; your guests will never dream you're dieting. This is best prepared one day in advance of serving. To serve 4, double all ingredients and bake for 45 minutes.

		Carbohydrates
8	ounces fillet of sole	0
1	egg white	tr
5	tablespoons heavy cream	2
1	tablespoon fresh dill weed or	
	½ tablespoon dried dill	0
	a pinch of cayenne pepper	0
½	teaspoon sea salt	0
6	center slices cucumber ⅛ inch thick	7
1	tablespoon mayonnaise thinned with	
2	teaspoons heavy cream	tr

Total	9
Total for 1	4½

Remove any remaining skin and bones from the fillets and cut the fish into 1-inch pieces. Place the uncooked fish and the egg white in the container of your blender and blend on low speed until smooth. Refrigerate for at least 1 hour.

Stir in heavy cream, 1 tablespoon at a time, beating thoroughly after each addition.

Beat in the dill, cayenne pepper and salt, and spoon the mixture into a greased Pyrex bowl 5 inches in diameter. Cover with waxed paper cut to fit.

Place this bowl in a cake pan of hot water and bake for 30–35 minutes in an oven preheated to 350°F. (or until the top feels firm).

Cool in the dish and then chill overnight.

To serve, turn the fish pâté onto a serving platter, cut into ½-inch slices and top with the cucumber slices.

Mix the mayonnaise and heavy cream and serve on the side.

Crunchy Chicken Balls

Whether you serve this as an hors d'oeuvre or a main course, you're certain to be delighted with these crunchy chicken bites.

		Carbohydrates
1	chicken breast, skinned and boned	0
1½	tablespoons red miso	5
⅛	teaspoon sea salt	0
4	water chestnuts	½
1	teaspoon whole wheat flour	1
1½	tablespoons almond kernel oil	0
	Total	6½

Grind the chicken breast or chop it finely.

Stir in the miso and salt.

Mince the water chestnuts and stir them, along with the flour, into the seasoned chicken meat. Form into small balls, using about 1 teaspoon of this mixture for each, and fry in hot oil for 3 or 4 minutes, or until brown on all sides.

Serve hot, dipped in a little soy sauce if you wish.

Deviled Crabmeat with Almonds

		Carbohydrates
3	ounces cooked crabmeat	1
1½	tablespoons butter	tr
⅛	teaspoon dry mustard	0
	sea salt to taste	0
1	tablespoon slivered, unblanched almonds	2
¼	cup heavy cream	1½
1	tablespoon mustard sprouts	0
	Total	4½

Pick over crabmeat and discard any hard bits of shell.
Melt butter in skillet and cook the crabmeat, dry mustard, salt and almonds until slightly browned, stirring occasionally.
Add the cream and cook for 2 minutes. Top with mustard sprouts.
Serve hot.

Liver Pâté

This is a very versatile as well as a tasty spread. Use it as a snack, a company spread, or a luncheon treat for you alone.

		Carbohydrates
3	ounces chicken livers	2½
1½	tablespoons butter	tr
1	hard-cooked egg, chopped	tr
1	tablespoon chopped onion	1
	a generous pinch each powdered cloves and nutmeg	0
½	clove garlic	0
2	teaspoons wheat germ	1½
	Total	5
	Total for 1 tablespoon	½

Trim the chicken livers and cut them into pieces.
Melt the butter in a skillet and sauté the livers until they are well done but not dry.
Add all ingredients to blender including any butter remaining in the pan.
Blend until smooth.
Place the pâté in a small, oiled dish and refrigerate until serving time.
Unmold on a lettuce leaf.
Use as a spread or an hors d'oeuvre.

Goat's Cheese Puffs

Absolutely luscious!

		Carbohydrates
5	tablespoons grated goat's cheese	tr
½	egg white	tr
1½	teaspoons wheat germ	1
½	cup safflower oil	0
	Total	1

Mix grated cheese and just enough egg white to make a stiff paste.
Roll into small balls and dip in wheat germ.
Fry in hot oil until the cheese puffs are golden brown.
Remove from oil, drain on paper towels and serve immediately.

Mushrooms with Dill Sauce

		Carbohydrates
4	large fresh mushrooms	4
2	tablespoons sour cream	1
1	scallion with 3 inches green top, minced	1
1	teaspoon fresh dill weed	0
	Total	6

Rinse or brush sand from mushrooms and thinly slice.
Mix sour cream, minced scallion and dill, and stir into mushroom slices.
Serve cold.

Mushrooms with Cashew Stuffing

Serves 4

		Carbohydrates
		Carbohydrates
4	fresh mushrooms	4
2	1-inch cubes goat's cheese	tr
8	raw cashew nuts	2
1	scallion with 3 inches green top	1
1	tablespoon heavy cream	0
	a pinch each of nutmeg and chili powder	0
	Total	7
	Total for 1	2

Rinse or brush sand from mushrooms.
Remove the stems and add them to your vegetable stock jar.
Finely chop the cheese, nuts and scallion.
Stir in the heavy cream and spices.
Stuff the mushrooms with this mixture and refrigerate.

Artichoke Bottoms with Sprouts

		Carbohydrates
1	cooked artichoke bottom	2
1	tablespoon sour cream	tr
	(or yoghurt mayonnaise, see page 33)	½
2	tablespoons alfalfa sprouts	0
½	teaspoon soy sauce	0
½	hard-cooked egg yolk	tr
	Total	2½

Spread artichoke bottom with sour cream (or yoghurt mayonnaise) and top with sprouts.
Sprinkle the soy sauce over the sprouts and top with half egg yolk placed round-side up.
Serve cold.

Marinated Mushrooms

		Carbohydrates
4	medium-sized fresh mushrooms	4
1	tablespoon tarragon vinegar	1
1½	tablespoons safflower oil	0
6	sprigs watercress	tr
2	teaspoons wheat germ	1
	Total	6

Rinse and dry mushrooms and carefully cut them into paper-thin slices.

Marinate mushroom slices for 1 hour in oil and vinegar. Discard the marinade.

Place the watercress on a salad plate and arrange the mushroom slices in two circles, stems pointing toward the center of the plate. Sprinkle with wheat germ.

Chill.

Serve cold.

Tongue and Melon Roll-Ups

		Carbohydrates
¼	ripe cantaloupe	7
¼	pound sliced cooked tongue	0
	fresh mint sprigs	0
	Total	7

Peel the cantaloupe and remove the seeds.
Cut into pieces ½ inch by 3 inches.
Wrap one piece melon and one sprig of mint with a slice of tongue.
Secure with a wooden pick.
Repeat until all ingredients are used.
Serve cold.

Shrimp-Stuffed Eggs with Asparagus

		Carbohydrates
1	hard-cooked egg	tr
2	cooked shrimp (shell and dark vein removed)	tr
½	clove garlic, crushed	0
1	tablespoon yoghurt mayonnaise (see page 33)	1½
¼	teaspoon dried dill	0
⅛	teaspoon sea salt	0
2	sprigs fresh dill weed	0
1	large lettuce leaf	1
4	spears cooked asparagus	2
	Total	4½

Split hard-cooked egg lengthwise and remove yolk. Force the yolk through a fine sieve.

Finely chop shrimp.

Mix sieved egg yolk, shrimp, garlic, 1 teaspoon of yoghurt mayonnaise, dill and sea salt.

Fill the egg whites with this mixture and decorate each half with a sprig of dill weed.

To serve, place lettuce leaf on plate. Arrange the stuffed, hard-cooked eggs and asparagus spears attractively on the lettuce leaf and decorate with remaining yoghurt mayonnaise.

Serve cold.

spreads
and sauces

Low Calorie
Spreads and Sauces

Fig and Nut Spread

		Calories
4	small figs	120
¼	cup chopped raw cashew nuts	150
1	small tart apple, cored	70
⅛	teaspoon cinnamon	0
	a generous pinch of cloves	0
	Total	340
	Total for 1 tablespoon	34

Finely chop or blend all ingredients.
Chill.

Lobster Spread

Spread this on whole grain bread, or heap on a lettuce leaf and enjoy it as a salad.

		Calories
1	scallion with 3 inches green top	4
½	pound cooked lobster	54
3	tablespoons yoghurt	24
1	teaspoon honey	22
3	tablespoons alfalfa sprouts	3
1	tablespoon wheat germ	15
¼	teaspoon sea salt	0
	Total	122
	Total for 1 tablespoon	8

Chop scallion and lobster.
Mix all ingredients.
Chill.
Use within 3 hours.

Oriental Egg Spread

		Calories
1	scallion with 3 inches green top	4
1	hard-cooked egg, shelled	75
1	slice fresh ginger root, peeled	1
1	teaspoon white miso	8
1	teaspoon yoghurt	3
	Total	91
	Total for 1 tablespoon	30

Finely chop scallion, hard-cooked egg and ginger root.
Mix miso and yoghurt.
Stir in egg mixture.
Chill.

Bean Curd Spread

Enough for 4 open-faced sandwiches

This is an unusual and really tasty spread for snacking, hors d'oeuvres or open-faced sandwiches.

		Calories
½	cup bean curd (see page 43)	80
3	scallions with 3 inches green top	12
½	green pepper, without pith or seeds	12
1	teaspoon miso paste	8
1	teaspoon lemon juice	1
	Total	113
	Total for 1 sandwich	28
	(not including bread)	

Mash the bean curd.
Mince the scallions and green pepper.
Mix all ingredients.
Chill.

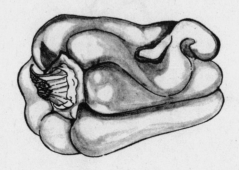

Fruit Spread

Enough for 3 open-faced sandwiches

		Calories
1	small pear	70
1	apple	70
2	tablespoons raisins	70
1½	tablespoons honey	99
1	teaspoon wheat germ	5
	Total	314
	Total for 1 sandwich	104
	(not including bread)	

Remove the seeds, core and stem of the pear and apple.
Grate the fruit. Chop the raisins. Mix all ingredients.
Refrigerate.

Carrot "Salmon" Spread

Enough for 4 open-faced sandwiches

Of course, nothing tastes exactly like salmon except salmon, but this comes close enough to warrant the name.

		Calories
3	medium-sized carrots	60
½	cup raw cashew nuts	380
1	tablespoon peanut butter	95
1	tablespoon yoghurt	8
1	teaspoon water	0
⅛	teaspoon sea salt	0
¼	teaspoon dill weed	0
	Total	543
	Total for 1 sandwich	136
	(not including bread)	

Wash the carrots and remove the stems and roots.
Chop the vegetables and the cashew nuts and place all ingredients in the container of your blender. Blend until fairly smooth, turning off the blender several times to push any carrot pieces down against the blades.
Chill.

Avocado Salad Dressing

Makes 8 tablespoons

Quick, easy and super-delicious, this lovely dressing makes a tasty guest-time dip, too!

		Calories
¼	avocado	92
2	tablespoons yoghurt	16
½	teaspoon lemon juice	0
½	teaspoon organic raw sugar	8
	Total	116
	Total for 1 tablespoon	14

Mash avocado, add yoghurt, lemon juice and sugar. Beat until smooth and rather fluffy.

Honey–Mint Yoghurt Sauce

A beautiful dressing for fruit salads or any lamb dish is this cool, exotic yoghurt concoction.

		Calories
1½	tablespoons honey	99
1	tablespoon chopped mint leaves	1
2	tablespoons water	0
½	cup plain yoghurt	60
	Total	160
	Total for 1 tablespoon	18

Simmer the honey, mint and water for a minute or two.
Cool and gently stir in the yoghurt.
Chill.

Sesame Seed Salad Dressing

		Calories
2	tablespoons sesame seeds	80
1	tablespoon lemon juice	5
1	teaspoon safflower oil	42
3	tablespoons vegetable stock	7
	a pinch each of curry and chili powders	0
	Total	134
	Total for 1 tablespoon	22

Place all ingredients in blender container and blend for 30 seconds.
Refrigerate.

Frozen Sweet
and Sour Horseradish Cream

Serves 4

Any platter of cold meat or fish becomes company fare when served with this frozen horseradish cream.

		Calories
½	horseradish root	5
2	apples, cored	140
1	tablespoon honey	66
1	cup yoghurt	120
⅛	teaspoon sea salt	0
	Total	331
	Total for 1 portion	83

Grate horseradish and apples. Mix with honey, yoghurt and salt. Freeze until mushy in a fairly deep glass bowl.
Stir the horseradish cream with a fork and refreeze.
To serve, arrange cold meat or fish on a platter and decorate with watercress.
Allow cream to soften slightly. Scoop out two balls of the frozen cream, place on the meat and serve immediately.

Cold Curry Sauce

Serves 2

Dip any raw vegetable in this spicy sauce for an instant appetizer.

		Calories
½	cup yoghurt	60
2	teaspoons honey	44
½	teaspoon lemon juice	0
¼	teaspoon curry powder	0
1	tablespoon finely chopped pumpkin seed kernels	31
	Total	135
	Total for 1	67

Mix all ingredients.
Chill well.

Marinade for Lamb

Use this marinade for lamb chops or for leg of lamb cut into 2-inch cubes.

Broil the meat until pink and serve hot with Honey–Mint Yoghurt (see page 77).

		Calories
½	cup lemon juice	40
3	tablespoons honey	198
¼	cup chopped fresh mint leaves	
	or 2 tablespoons dried mint	3
2	bay leaves, crumbled	0

Total 241

However, only about 1/5 of the
marinade adheres to the meat
Total with marinade discarded 48
(not including calorie count of lamb)

Mix all ingredients and pour over meat.
Refrigerate.
Marinate for 3 days, turning meat occasionally.

Lovely Flower Syrup

This is a beautiful syrup to sweeten nearly anything.

		Calories
1	cup water	0
½	cup fresh orange juice	112
1	cup organic raw sugar	816
1	tablespoon Lovely Flower Tea	0
½	teaspoon lemon juice	0
	Total	928
	Total for 1 tablespoon	46

Boil until the liquid is reduced by half.
Pour into a clear glass jar. Do not strain.
Refrigerate.
Lovely Flower Tea may be ordered from Rocky Hollow Herb Farm, Sussex, New Jersey; or pick and dry your own flowers of elder, rose petals, yarrow, lavender and blue malva. Add camomile and sassafras if desired.

Low Carbohydrate
Spreads and Sauces

Dill Butter

Use this versatile butter as a spread or as a topping for fresh-cooked vegetables.

		Carbohydrates
¼	cup butter	tr
2	teaspoons minced fresh dill weed	0
1	teaspoon lemon juice	tr
1	teaspoon minced chives	tr
	Total	tr
	Total for 1 tablespoon	tr

Place all ingredients in blender container and blend until smooth.
Chill.

Mushroom Spread

This recipe makes enough for 3 open-faced sandwiches, but it is also delicious when served as an hors d'oeuvre.

		Carbohydrates
1	cup coarsely chopped mushrooms	8
1	small onion, chopped	10
2	teaspoons butter	tr
1	tablespoon sour cream	½
⅛	teaspoon sea salt	0
	Total	18½
	Total for 1 sandwich	6
	(not including bread)	

Sauté mushrooms and onion in butter until onion is transparent. Stir in sour cream and salt.
Serve hot or cold.

Sprout Spread

Sweet and hot and crunchy is this super-nutritious spread.

		Carbohydrates
1	tablespoon alfalfa sprouts	0
1	tablespoon winter wheat sprouts	0
1	tablespoon mustard sprouts	0
1	hard-cooked egg, chopped	tr
1	scallion with 3 inches green top, chopped	1
1	tablespoon sour cream	½
¼	teaspoon sea salt	0
	Total	1½
	Total for 1 tablespoon	tr

Gently mix all ingredients.
Chill and serve within 3 hours.

Green Spread

		Carbohydrates
¼	cup watercress without stems (save stems for vegetable stock)	0
½	medium-sized cucumber, peeled	3½
1	scallion with 3 inches green top	1
¼	cup winter wheat sprouts	2
1	tablespoon yoghurt	1
1	tablespoon cream cheese	tr
½	clove garlic, crushed	0
	Total	7½
	Total for 1 tablespoon	tr

Finely chop watercress, cucumber, scallion and sprouts.
Mix the yoghurt, cream cheese and garlic.
Gently stir the greens into the cheese mixture.
Chill. Serve cold.

Cashew–Cheese Spread

For one of the best hot sandwiches ever, simply spread this on one slice of whole grain bread, grill, and top with cold avocado slices.

		Carbohydrates
2	1-inch cubes goat's cheese	tr
6	raw cashew nuts	1½
1	scallion with 3 inches green top	1
	a generous pinch each of curry powder and nutmeg	0
	Total	2½

Grate or finely chop cheese, nuts and scallion.
Mix in spices.

Yoghurt Sour Cream Sauce

Makes approximately 8 tablespoons

		Carbohydrates
¼	cup yoghurt	3
¼	cup sour cream	2
1	scallion with 3 inches green top	1
¼	medium-sized tomato	2
½	teaspoon each caraway and poppy seeds	0
1	teaspoon butter	tr
½	clove garlic, crushed	0
⅛	teaspoon cayenne	0
	Total	8
	Total for 1 tablespoon	1

Mix yoghurt and sour cream.
Mince scallion and tomato.
Brown the caraway and poppy seeds in butter.
Mix all ingredients.
Refrigerate.
Serve cold.

Salty Peanut Dip

Serves 2

Celery and squash slices become something special when dipped in this interesting sauce.

		Carbohydrates
3	tablespoons natural organic peanut butter	9
1	tablespoon soy sauce	1
1	teaspoon lemon juice	tr
½	clove garlic, crushed	0
3	tablespoons heavy cream	½
	Total	10½
	Total for 1	5

Mix peanut butter, soy sauce, lemon juice and garlic together over a low flame.
Stir in cream.
Serve hot.

Cheese–Avocado Dip

Dip crisp, raw zucchini and summer squash slices into this unusual sauce.

		Carbohydrates
¼	ripe avocado	3
1	1-inch cube goat's cheese	tr
½	clove garlic, crushed	0
2	tablespoons yoghurt	2
2	tablespoons sour cream	1
¼	teaspoon sea salt	0
	a generous pinch chili powder	0
1	tablespoon chopped unblanched almonds	2
	Total	8
	Total for 1 tablespoon	1

Peel and mash the avocado.
Grate the cheese.
Mix the garlic, yoghurt, sour cream, sea salt and chili powder.
Stir in the avocado, cheese and almonds.
Chill.
Serve cold.

Sour Cream Sauce

Try this on any raw or cooked green vegetable that needs dressing up.

		Carbohydrates
½	tablespoon poppy seeds	0
½	tablespoon safflower oil	0
½	tablespoon butter	tr
½	tablespoon sesame seeds	0
½	clove garlic, crushed	0
¼	cup sour cream	2
¼	teaspoon sea salt	0
	Total	2
	Total for 1 tablespoon	tr

Toast the poppy seeds for 2 minutes over medium heat. Add the safflower oil, butter and sesame seeds, and stir over low heat for 3 minutes more.
Mix the garlic, sour cream and sea salt, and add this to the toasted seeds.
Stir over low heat until the cream is hot.
Do not allow the mixture to boil.

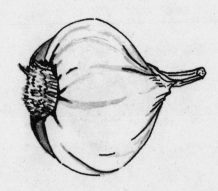

Apple–Horseradish Sauce

Serves 2

Cold sliced beef, turkey, chicken or lamb all become very special when topped with this piquant sauce.

		Carbohydrates
¼	horseradish root	0
½	apple, cored	9
1	tablespoon yoghurt	8
3	tablespoons sour cream	1½
⅛	teaspoon sea salt	0
	Total	18½
	Total for 1	9

Grate horseradish and apple, mix with remaining ingredients and chill.

soups

Low Calorie Soups

Hot Cucumber Soup

		Calories
1	teaspoon butter	33
½	cucumber	15
1	scallion with 3 inches green top	4
1	cup chicken stock	2
¼	teaspoon vegetable salt seasoning	0
	a pinch of nutmeg	0
1	tablespoon yoghurt	8
1	teaspoon chopped mint leaves	0
	Total	62

Melt butter in pan.
Peel half cucumber and cut in half lengthwise. Remove the seeds and cut the remaining cucumber into thin slices. Sauté for 2 minutes.
Chop scallion and add it, along with the stock and spices, to the pan.
Simmer for 5 minutes.
Serve hot topped with yoghurt and chopped mint leaves.

Cabbage Soup

Serves 2

This takes rather a long time to cook but requires very little work. Still, if you are devoting the time to it, why not make at least a double portion? It chills well.

		Calories
2	cups water	0
¼	cabbage, with hard stem removed	30
1	small onion, chopped	30
⅛	teaspoon sea salt	0
1½	teaspoons sesame butter	28
	Total	88

Bring the water to a boil.
Add the cabbage, onion and sea salt.
Reduce heat and simmer, partially covered, for 50–60 minutes, or until the cabbage is tender.
Stir in the sesame butter.
Serve hot.

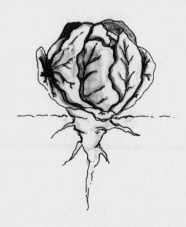

Healthy Onion Soup

		Calories
1	small onion	30
1	teaspoon butter	33
1	cup beef stock	22
½	teaspoon nutritional yeast	3
½	clove garlic, crushed	0
1	1-inch cube goat's cheese, grated	30
	Total	118

Peel the onion and cut into ¼-inch slices.
Separate the slices into rings.
Melt the butter in a skillet and sauté the onion rings until tender.
Add the stock, yeast and crushed garlic, and boil for several minutes.
Place the soup in a bowl, top with grated cheese and serve immediately.

Buttermilk Soup

		Calories
½	cucumber	15
1	cup buttermilk	90
½	teaspoon lemon juice	0
1	teaspoon honey	22
½	teaspoon fresh dill	0
1	teaspoon fresh mint leaves	0
⅛	teaspoon sea salt	0
	Total	127

Peel and chop cucumber.
Place all ingredients in blender.
Blend until smooth.
Chill.
Serve cold topped with a mint leaf or two.

Watercress Soup

		Calories
½	bunch watercress	2
1	small potato	60
1	small onion	30
2	cups chicken stock	4
1	tablespoon whole wheat flour	16
2	teaspoons yoghurt	6
⅛	teaspoon sea salt	0
	a pinch of nutmeg	0
	Total	118

While you wash the watercress, keep an eye open for snails.
They seem to love this nutritious plant as much as we do.
Discard the dark, wilted leaves and any presumptuous snails.
Peel and slice the potato and onion and cook in chicken stock
until tender.
Chop the watercress and add to the vegetables and stock. Cook
for 15 minutes.
Rub the soup through a sieve (or blend and strain it).
Mix the flour with a little water and the yoghurt and spices.
Blend this mixture into the soup.
Stir over medium heat until thick.
Serve hot.

Carrot Soup

Filling enough to take the place of lunch or to make a gourmet dinner even more special is this rich and nourishing soup.

		Calories
½	tablespoon butter	50
2	medium-sized carrots	40
1	small tomato	25
½	cup chicken stock	1
¼	cup water	0
¼	teaspoon nutritional yeast	2
¼	teaspoon organic raw sugar	4
	a pinch of sea salt	0
1	cup milk	160
½	teaspoon finely chopped parsley	0
1	teaspoon alfalfa sprouts	0
	Total	282

Melt the butter in a skillet.
Peel the carrots and thinly slice them. Add the carrots to the butter and cook over low heat for 5 minutes.
Chop the tomato, add to the carrots and sauté for 2 minutes.
Heat the stock with the water, yeast, sugar and sea salt. Pour into the carrot mixture, cover and simmer for 30 minutes.
Stir in the milk, reheat, top with parsley and sprouts and serve immediately.

Sweet and Sour Cabbage Soup

		Calories
¼	cabbage, with hard stem removed	30
1	small onion	30
1	small apple	50
½	cup tomato juice	22
	a pinch of allspice	0
2	teaspoons lemon juice	2
1½	teaspoons honey	33
1½	cups heated chicken stock	3
	Total	170

Shred the cabbage. Peel and chop the onion. Core the apple and cut into slices.
Place all ingredients in the heated chicken stock.
Simmer for 30 minutes or until the soup is fairly thick.
Serve hot.

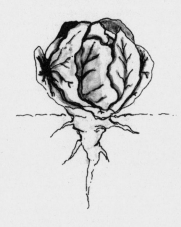

Hot Tomato and Yoghurt Soup

		Calories
1	large ripe tomato	50
1	small onion, peeled	30
1	teaspoon butter	33
¼	cup chicken stock	0
½	teaspoon honey	11
½	cup milk	80
2	tablespoons yoghurt	16
¼	teaspoon basil leaves	0
	sea salt and pepper to taste	0
	Total	220

Chop the tomato and onion and sauté in butter until the onion is transparent.
Add a tablespoon or two of stock if necessary, to keep the vegetables from browning.
Add the stock and honey and simmer for 5 minutes.
Stir in remaining ingredients and continue simmering for 3 minutes more.
Serve hot.

Low Carbohydrate Soups

Oriental Sprout Soup

		Carbohydrates
1	cup basic chicken stock	1
1	egg	tr
2	teaspoons water	0
2	teaspoons soy sauce	0
2	tablespoons winter wheat sprouts	0
	Total	1

Heat stock to simmering. Beat the egg with the water.
Use a spoon to dribble the egg into the simmering soup.
Stir in the soy sauce.
Chop the sprouts and sprinkle them on top of the soup.
Serve hot.

Egg Drop Soup

		Carbohydrates
½	cup ground raw veal	0
½	teaspoon soy sauce	0
⅛	teaspoon dulse	0
1	tablespoon soy oil	0
1	cup chicken stock	1
¼	cup alfalfa sprouts	1
½	cup spinach	3
1	egg	tr
1	teaspoon water	0
	Total	4

Mix ground veal and soy sauce.

Crumble or cut the dulse into tiny pieces.

Fry meat, soy sauce and dulse in oil over medium heat for 3 minutes.

Add chicken stock and simmer while you chop sprouts and spinach.

Add these chopped vegetables to the soup and boil for 3 minutes.

Beat the egg and water in a cup.

Remove the soup from the heat and beat in the egg.

Simmer for 30 seconds, without boiling, and serve immediately.

Goat's Cheese Soup

		Carbohydrates
1	teaspoon butter	tr
½	cup heavy cream	3½
¼	teaspoon nutritional yeast	0
½	clove garlic, crushed	0
½	cup grated goat's cheese	tr
1	egg yolk	tr
1	tablespoon mustard sprouts	0
1	teaspoon chopped walnuts	tr
	Total	3½

Bring water to a boil in the bottom of a double boiler.

Place the butter, ¼ cup of cream, nutritional yeast and crushed garlic in the top half of the double boiler.

Heat slightly. Add the cheese and stir over low heat until melted.

Beat remaining ¼ cup of cream with the egg yolk, add to the cheese mixture and stir for several minutes.

Do not allow to boil.

Serve immediately, topped with sprouts and nuts.

Cold Senegalese Soup with Yoghurt

		Carbohydrates
1	cup chicken stock	1
¼	cup finely chopped cooked chicken	0
1	egg yolk	tr
¼	cup cream	2
¼	teaspoon curry powder	0
1	teaspoon yoghurt	0
2	watercress leaves	0
	Total	3

Heat the chicken stock and the chicken.
Beat together the egg yolk, cream and curry powder.
Add the egg yolk mixture to the stock and stir over low heat until the soup is just thickened.
Do not boil or the egg will curdle.
Cool the soup and chill in the refrigerator.
Serve cold topped with yoghurt and watercress.

Lettuce Soup

		Carbohydrates
1¼	cups chicken stock (page 37)	1
½	cup shredded iceberg lettuce	6
1	egg yolk	tr
1	tablespoon sunflower seed kernels	1
1	teaspoon chopped parsley	0
⅛	teaspoon sea salt	0
	Total	8

Bring the stock to a boil. Stir in the shredded lettuce and let boil for 3 minutes.

Beat egg yolk in a bowl and gradually beat into it the lettuce and stock.

Stir in the remaining ingredients and serve immediately.

Chicken Soup with Cheese Squares

Italian in origin, this interesting soup is both tasty and healthful.

		Carbohydrates
4	tablespoons ricotta or cottage cheese	2
1	egg	tr
1	egg yolk	tr
½	teaspoon wheat germ	tr
	a pinch each of nutmeg and sea salt	0
1	cup basic chicken stock (page 37)	1
	Total	3

Place ricotta or cottage cheese in blender container.
Beat together the egg and egg yolk. Place half of the beaten egg in the blender along with the wheat germ, nutmeg and sea salt.
Blend until fairly smooth. Place cheese paste in an oiled glass baking dish; place the dish in a pan of hot water and bake until firm (approximately 20 minutes) in an oven preheated to 300°F.
Cool the paste and cut into 1-inch squares.
Heat the stock to boiling and beat in the remaining raw egg. Place the cheese cubes in a soup dish and pour the stock over them.
Serve immediately.

Chilled Shrimp and Avocado Soup

Try this for a summertime lunch!

		Carbohydrates
1	cup ice-cold basic chicken stock (see page 37)	1
½	cucumber	3½
¼	avocado	3
2	large, cooked shrimp	tr
1	scallion with 3 inches green top	1
1	teaspoon soy sauce	0
	a pinch each of powdered cloves and chili powder	0
¼	teaspoon vegetable salt seasoning	0
1	tablespoon yoghurt	1
	Total	9½

Place chicken stock in bowl. Refrigerate.
Peel and chop cucumber, avocado and shrimp. Mince scallion.
To serve, stir cucumber, avocado, shrimp, scallion, soy sauce and spices into the chilled chicken stock.
Top with yoghurt.
Serve immediately.

Asparagus and Egg Luncheon Soup

This nutrition-packed soup is a lunch in itself.

		Carbohydrates
¾	cup beef stock	4½
½	teaspoon nutritional yeast	0
	a small piece of dulse	0
6	asparagus spears	3
½	tablespoon butter	tr
1	egg	tr
1	teaspoon alfalfa sprouts	0
	Total	7½

Heat stock, yeast and dulse.
Wash and peel asparagus spears and simmer them in the stock
for 5 minutes.
Melt the butter in a skillet and fry the egg as you like it.
Place the soup and asparagus spears in a bowl.
Top with the fried egg and alfalfa sprouts.
Serve immediately.

meat, fish and egg dishes

Low Calorie Meat,
Fish and Egg Dishes

Diced Chicken Breast with Peas

		Calories
½	chicken breast, boned and skinned	80
½	tablespoon soybean (or other) oil	62
2	large stalks celery	10
3	scallions with 3 inches green top	12
3	tablespoons fresh baby peas	36
2	tablespoons soy sauce	20
4	tablespoons water	0
½	teaspoon whole wheat flour	2
2	tablespoons alfalfa sprouts	2
	Total	224

Cut chicken into 1-inch pieces.
Heat oil in skillet.
Wash, dry and cut celery into twigs, 2 inches by ¼ inch. Remove root and excess top from scallions and cut them diagonally into 1-inch pieces.
Stir the chicken pieces in the hot oil for 1 minute.
Add the celery twigs, scallions and peas and stir-fry for 3 minutes more.
Pour the soy sauce and 2 tablespoons of water into the pan.
Cover and cook over very low heat for 5 minutes, adding a little more water if necessary to prevent sticking.
Mix the water and wheat flour; add to the chicken mixture and stir until the sauce thickens. Garnish with alfalfa sprouts.
Serve hot.

Cold Sliced Chicken with Yoghurt

This interesting dish makes an excellent company luncheon.
Simply multiply by the number of guests, arrange the chicken
on a platter, and decorate with the sauce.

		Calories
4	thin slices (2 ounces) cold cooked chicken breast without skin	122
2	tablespoons yoghurt	16
½	hard-cooked egg, chopped	37
1	teaspoon grated horseradish	1
1	scallion, minced	4
	Total	180

Slice chicken and refrigerate.
Mix yoghurt, hard-cooked egg, horseradish and scallion.
Top chicken slices with yoghurt mixture.
Serve very cold.

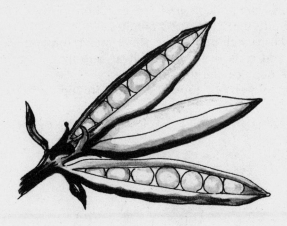

Chicken with Curried Fruit Sauce

		Calories
½	chicken breast	80
1	teaspoon safflower oil (or other unhydrogenated oil)	42
1	orange, medium-sized	60
	a generous pinch each curry powder, organic raw sugar, sea salt and cinnamon	0
4	dried apricot halves	39
2	raw cashew nuts	20
¼	teaspoon cornstarch	4
2	tablespoons water	0
	Total	245

Pull skin from chicken breast.

Heat oil in a small skillet and brown chicken on both sides.

Remove pan from the heat and stir in the juice from the orange, the sugar and the spices.

Cover and cook breast-side down over *low* heat until breast meat is no longer pink, adding water if necessary.

Cut each of the apricots in 4 pieces. Chop the nuts. Add the fruit and nuts and cook for 3 minutes.

Mix the cornstarch and water, stir it into the orange sauce in the pan and cook over medium heat, stirring constantly until the sauce bubbles and thickens.

Serve the chicken hot, topped with the fruited sauce.

Chicken with Mushrooms

		Calories
1	chicken breast, boned	160
2½	tablespoons soy sauce	25
1	tablespoon organic raw sugar	51
2	tablespoons water	0
1	clove garlic, crushed	0
2	large mushrooms	20
5	water chestnuts	30
1	tablespoon almond kernel oil	125
	Total	411

Cut chicken into 1½-inch squares.

Mix soy sauce, sugar, water and garlic, and marinate chicken pieces in this for 45 minutes.

Slice mushrooms and water chestnuts. Heat oil in a Teflon skillet and fry the chicken pieces for 5 minutes, retaining the marinade. Stir in the mushrooms and water chestnuts and fry for 5 minutes more. Add the reserved marinade and stir until sauce is quite thick.

Serve hot.

Turkey or Chicken Chow Mein

		Calories
½	cup (2 ounces) cooked chicken, cut in cubes	246
½	medium onion	20
2	scallions with 3 inches green top	8
½	cup sliced mushrooms	32
½	cup sliced celery	7½
1	cup chicken stock	2
1	tablespoon soy sauce	10
1	teaspoon cornstarch	17
½	cup bean sprouts	8
1	tablespoon slivered almonds	53
2	tablespoons cooked brown rice	25
	Total	428½

Measure chicken and set aside. Chop onion and scallions.
Simmer onion, scallions, mushrooms and celery in the stock for 5 minutes.
Stir in soy sauce and cornstarch mixed with a little water.
Cook, stirring, for 4 minutes.
Add chicken, bean sprouts, almonds and cooked rice.
Stir over medium heat for 1 minute more.
Serve hot.

Skewered Chicken Livers and Apple with Honey

		Calories
6	ounces chicken livers	216
1	tablespoon honey	66
1	tablespoon soy sauce	10
	a pinch of powdered anise	0
⅛	teaspoon nutmeg	0
1	McIntosh apple	70

Total	362
Total with excess marinade discarded	306

Preheat the broiler.

Wash the livers and drain them on paper towels.

Mix the honey, soy sauce and spices, and marinate the livers for 15 minutes.

Core the apple, cut it into 1-inch chunks. Dip the pieces in the marinade.

Thread the fruit and livers alternately on a skewer, beginning and ending with an apple chunk.

Broil, turning the skewer several times, until the livers are cooked but still slightly pink in the centers.

Serve immediately.

Chicken Livers Miso

		Calories
5	ounces chicken livers	180
1	teaspoon butter	33
1	teaspoon red miso paste	8
1	scallion with 3 inches green top	4
2	teaspoons yoghurt	6
	Total	231

Rinse and dry chicken livers.
Melt butter in skillet.
Sauté chicken livers until they are slightly pink inside.
Stir in miso paste.
Chop the scallion.
To serve, spoon livers and sauce onto plate, top with yoghurt and chopped scallion.
Serve immediately.

Sweet and Salty Skewered Veal

		Calories
6	ounces lean veal	360
1	tablespoon soy sauce	10
2	teaspoons raw buckwheat honey	44
1	scallion with 3 inches green top	4
	Total	418
	Total with marinade discarded	364

Cut the veal into 1-inch cubes.

Mix the soy sauce and honey and marinate the meat in this for 20 minutes. Mince the scallion.

A quarter of an hour before serving time, discard marinade, roll the veal cubes in the chopped scallion and thread them on a skewer. Broil under a high flame until the cubes are brown on the outside but not dried out, approximately 5 minutes on each side.

Serve sizzling hot.

Veal Chops with Mushrooms

Serves 2

		Calories
2	small veal chops (loin without tail)	528
2	teaspoons butter	66
4	mushrooms	32
1	small onion	30
1	small tomato	25
½	cup vegetable stock (see page 38)	40
½	clove garlic, crushed	0
	a pinch of thyme	0
	sea salt and pepper to taste	0
	Total	721
	Total for 1	360

Trim the excess fat from the veal chops, melt the butter in a skillet and brown the meat on both sides.

Slice the mushrooms. Chop the onion and the tomato.

Remove the veal chops and sauté the vegetables for 5 minutes, stirring frequently.

Return the meat to the pan, add the remaining ingredients, cover tightly and simmer for 1 hour.

Serve hot.

Baked Lamb Curry

		Calories
6	ounces lean lamb	312
2	teaspoons butter	66
½	medium onion	20
1	apple	70
½	beaten egg	38
1	tablespoon milk	10
⅛	teaspoon curry powder, or more if you like your curry hot	0
	sea salt and pepper to taste	0
	Total	516

Chop the lamb into ½-inch cubes.
Melt the butter in a skillet and sauté the lamb for 5 minutes, stirring frequently.
Grate the onion and the apple.
Beat together the egg, apple, onion, milk, curry powder, sea salt and pepper. Mix this with the cooled lamb.
Place in a small, greased, ovenproof dish and bake for 35–40 minutes in an oven preheated to 350°F.
Serve hot.

Sweet and Sour Beef and Vegetables

If your calorie count permits, serve this with a little brown rice.

		Calories
4	ounces flank steak	160
1	teaspoon apricot kernel oil	42
1	medium-sized green pepper	15
1	small carrot	20
1	medium-sized onion	40
1	medium-sized tomato	35
¼	cup bean sprouts	4
¼	cup beef stock (page 39)	5
1	clove garlic	0
⅛	teaspoon ginger	0
1	tablespoon soy sauce	10
1	tablespoon vinegar	2
2	teaspoons organic raw sugar	34
½	teaspoon cornstarch	9
	Total	376

Cut flank steak into ¼-inch slices. Heat oil in Teflon skillet. Quickly brown meat on each side. This should take only a few seconds. Do not overcook.

Cut green pepper into 1-inch pieces. Thinly slice carrot, onion and tomato.

Remove the meat from the pan, add the green pepper, carrot and onion, and cook over medium heat for 5 minutes. Stir in all ingredients except meat and cornstarch. Simmer for 4 minutes. Mix the cornstarch with 2 tablespoons of water and add, with the beef, to the ingredients in the pan. Stir constantly for 2 minutes more.

Serve hot on cooked brown rice.

Smothered Onions
with Beef and Bulghour

		Calories
1	medium onion	40
3	ounces chopped lean sirloin	173
2	tablespoons raw slivered almonds	106
1	teaspoon honey	22
2	tablespoons ketchup	30
1	teaspoon soy sauce	3
2	tablespoons basic bulghour recipe (see page 41)	26
	a sprinkle of nutmeg, sweet basil and cloves	0
	Total	400

Peel onion and cut it in half.
Brown chopped sirloin over high heat.
Add nuts and onions and fry 2 minutes more.
Stir in remaining ingredients, place in a casserole, cover and bake for 30 minutes in an oven preheated to 350°F.

123

Shrimp and Rice Casserole

Shrimp and rice—an old standby made unusually delicious by the use of brown rice.

		Calories
1	scallion with 3 inches green top	4
1	1-inch cube cheese	70
2	tablespoons leftover cooked brown rice	25
3	ounces cooked shrimp	75
1	egg	75
	sea salt and pepper to taste	0
	Total	249

Chop scallion. Grate cheese. Combine scallion, grated cheese, rice and shrimp. Beat egg, salt and pepper. Fold egg into rice mixture and place in a small, greased casserole.
Set the casserole in a pan of hot water and bake for 25 minutes in an oven preheated to 350°F.
Serve hot.

Shrimp Fried Brown Rice

		Calories
2	strips bacon	100
2	mushrooms	16
1	scallion	4
3	ounces cooked shrimp	75
3	tablespoons cooked brown rice	38
1	teaspoon soy sauce	3
1	egg	75
	Total	311

Mince bacon and fry over high heat for 1 minute.
Wash, trim and thinly slice mushrooms and scallion.
Peel, devein and split shrimp in half lengthwise.
Add the mushrooms, scallion and shrimp to the bacon and stir-fry for 6 minutes.
Stir in the rice and soy sauce and fry 3 minutes more.
Beat the egg and pour it over the shrimp and rice. Stir over medium heat until the egg is set but not dry.
Serve immediately.

Jambalaya Fish Stew

Serves 2

		Calories
½	slice slab bacon (about 2 ounces)	354
1	small onion	30
½	green pepper	12
1	stalk celery	5
1	tomato	25
2	cups chicken stock (see page 37)	4
1	tablespoon cornmeal	26
¼	cup water	0
1	teaspoon organic raw sugar	17
1	teaspoon nutritional yeast	7
1	teaspoon minced dulse or other seaweed	0
⅛	teaspoon each dill, basil, oregano, fennel seed	0
4	shrimp in the shell	100
½	large fillet of sole (3 ounces)	78
	Total	658
	Total for 1	329

Cut bacon from rind and slice into ¼-inch pieces. Fry over medium heat for 5 minutes. Peel the onion and remove the seeds from the green pepper.

Chop the onion, celery and green pepper and add them to the bacoñ. Sauté until the onion is golden.

Peel and chop the tomato and add it, with the stock, to the sautéed vegetables.

Soak the cornmeal in water for 5 minutes. Add the cornmeal, sugar, yeast, dulse, spices and shrimp. Cover the stew and simmer for 20 minutes.

Remove any small bones or skin from the fish and cut it in 1½-inch squares. Add the fish to the stew and boil for 4 minutes. Serve hot.

Crabmeat Omelet

This omelet tastes equally delicious hot at lunchtime or as a cold side dish with Sushi, (page 44).

		Calories
2	ounces cooked crabmeat	60
2	tablespoons frozen peas	20
1	scallion with 2 inches green top	4
1	egg	75
1	teaspoon safflower oil	42
2	teaspoons soy sauce	6
	Total	207

Place the crabmeat and frozen peas in a bowl.
Cut the root from the scallion and mince it.
Mix all ingredients except the oil and the soy sauce.
Heat the oil in a small skillet and cook the omelet, turning once.
Cut the omelet into squares, top with soy sauce and serve hot or cold.

Bacon, Egg and Potato Casserole

For luncheon or dinner, this fabulous combination hits the spot
. . . and multiplied by the proper number, it makes a fabulous
family repast.

		Calories
1	slice bacon	47
½	small tomato	13
1	scallion with 3 inches green top	4
1	1-inch cube cheese	70
1	teaspoon chopped parsley	0
2	tablespoons diced boiled potatoes	21
1	egg	75
	a pinch of oregano	0
	sea salt and pepper to taste	0
	Total	230

Chop bacon, tomato and scallion.
Sauté bacon until crisp. Add tomato and scallion and cook 1
minute over medium heat.
Grate cheese. Combine bacon, tomato, scallion, parsley, grated
cheese and diced potatoes.
Beat the egg, oregano, sea salt and pepper. Fold egg into potato
mixture and place in a small, greased casserole.
Set the casserole in a pan of hot water and bake for 25 minutes
in an oven preheated to 350°F.
Serve hot.

Baked Egg with Mushrooms

		Calories
4	medium-sized fresh mushrooms	32
1	tablespoon butter	100
½	clove garlic	0
½	medium-sized tomato, chopped	17
1	large scallion, chopped	4
¼	cup chicken stock	0
	a pinch each of tarragon and chervil	0
2	teaspoons minced fresh parsley	1
2	eggs	150
	Total	304

Wash the mushrooms thoroughly and separate the caps from the stems.

Cut the caps into quarters and chop the stems.

Melt the butter in the pan, add the mushrooms and the garlic clove and fry over medium-high heat, stirring frequently.

When mushrooms are nicely browned, remove the garlic and add the chopped tomato, scallion, chicken stock, tarragon and chervil.

Wash the parsley thoroughly, mince it, and stir it into the mushroom mixture.

Simmer until most of the liquid has disappeared.

Place the mushroom mixture in a glass baking dish and push aside the vegetables to form a well. Break the eggs into this well and bake in an oven preheated to 350°F., 10 minutes for soft, 15 minutes for medium or 20 minutes for a hard egg.

Serve at once.

Low Carbohydrate Meat, Fish and Egg Dishes

Cold Broiled Chicken on Watercress

If you're expecting guests, try this cook-ahead dinner.

		Carbohydrates
1	tablespoon safflower oil	0
1	tablespoon lemon juice	1
¼	teaspoon dry mustard	0
1	chicken leg and thigh (or breast, if you prefer)	0
2	tablespoons vinaigrette dressing (see page 131)	0
5	sprigs watercress	0
	Total	1
	Total without marinade	0

Mix the oil, lemon juice and dry mustard. Marinate the chicken in this for 2 hours, turning occasionally.
Broil under high heat for 5 minutes on each side, then lower heat and continue cooking until done.
Baste every 5 minutes with marinade.
Cool and chill.
To serve, dip watercress in vinaigrette dressing, shake, arrange on serving plate and top with the chilled chicken.

Vinaigrette Dressing

		Carbohydrates
1	tablespoon olive oil	0
2	teaspoons lemon juice	0
⅛	teaspoon each sea salt, natural organic sugar,	
	dry mustard and pepper	0
	Total	0

Mix well.

Use to flavor watercress sprigs and also as a sauce for the chicken if desired.

Steamed Chicken Breast

. . . almost like Mother used to make . . .

		Carbohydrates
1	chicken breast, halved	0
2	teaspoons whole wheat flour	2
	a pinch each of thyme and chili powder	0
	sea salt and pepper to taste	0
1½	tablespoons almond kernel (or other) oil	0
	Total	2

Pull the skin from the chicken. Mix the flour, thyme, chili powder, sea salt and pepper. Rub the chicken breast with this. Heat the oil in a frying pan and, when hot, brown the chicken on all sides.
Turn with the breast-side up, cover and steam over a very low flame for 20 minutes or until done.
Serve hot.

Soy Fried Chicken

If you have an electric skillet you can prepare this tasty chicken in front of your guests.

		Carbohydrates
1	chicken breast	0
2	tablespoons soy sauce	3
1	tablespoon lemon juice	1
2	teaspoons organic raw sugar	8
1½	teaspoons cornstarch	3
3	tablespoons almond kernel oil	0
	Total	15
	Total with marinade poured off	7

Use a meat cleaver to chop the chicken, with the bones, into 2-inch pieces.

Mix soy sauce, lemon juice and sugar, and marinate chicken pieces in this for at least 1 hour.

Drain chicken and work the cornstarch into the meat with your fingers.

Heat oil to 350°F. and fry the chicken pieces 6 minutes on each side or until brown and cooked through.

Serve immediately.

Chicken Livers with Sour Cream

		Carbohydrates
7	ounces chicken livers	6
2	teaspoons butter	tr
	a pinch of nutmeg	0
	sea salt to taste	0
2½	tablespoons sour cream	1
½	teaspoon fresh dill weed (or ¼	
	teaspoon dried dill)	0
	Total	7

Rinse and dry chicken livers.
Sauté in melted butter until livers are slightly pink inside.
Add nutmeg, sea salt, sour cream and dill weed.
Stir for a few seconds until the cream is warm. Do not boil.
Serve immediately.

Skewered Veal with Rosemary

		Carbohydrates
8	ounces lean veal	0
2	teaspoons butter	tr
1	teaspoon rosemary leaves	0
¼	teaspoon thyme leaves	0
	Total	tr

Cut the veal into 1-inch cubes, dip in melted butter, roll in rosemary and thyme and thread the meat on a skewer.
Broil under a high flame until the cubes are brown on the outside but not dried out, approximately 5 minutes on each side.
Serve sizzling hot.

Sautéed Lamb Kidneys

		Carbohydrates
6	ounces lamb kidneys	0
1	tablespoon butter or oil	tr
1	tablespoon cornmeal	5
	a pinch each of nutmeg and thyme	0
	sea salt to taste	0
1	scallion with 3 inches green top	1
	Total	6

Remove skin and core from kidneys.
Cut the kidneys into thin slices and sprinkle with cornmeal, nutmeg, thyme and sea salt.
Sauté in butter for 5 minutes, stirring constantly.
Chop scallion, stir it into the kidneys, and serve immediately.

Cold Sliced Lamb with Yoghurt

		Carbohydrates
4	slices cold lamb	0
2	tablespoons yoghurt	2
½	clove garlic	0
1	tablespoon minced parsley	0
1	scallion	1
	Total	3

Slice lamb, place on serving plate and refrigerate.
Mix yoghurt, crushed garlic, minced parsley and scallion.
Top lamb with yoghurt mixture and serve very cold.

Lamb Chops with Mint

		Carbohydrates
2	loin lamb chops	0
1	teaspoon dried mint	0
2	teaspoons butter	tr
	wedge of lemon	3
	Total	3

Rinse meat and dry well.
Press dried mint leaves into both sides of the chops. Refrigerate for at least 1 hour.
Melt butter in skillet and fry chops to desired degree of doneness.
Serve hot with a wedge of lemon.

Lamb and Couscous Casserole

Here's another Middle East adaptation that will help make your dieting a pleasure.

		Carbohydrates
2	tablespoons ground, cooked lamb	0
1	tablespoon butter	tr
1	scallion with 3 inches green top	1
1	1-inch cube cheese	tr
2	tablespoons cooked couscous	5
1	egg	tr
	a pinch of thyme	0
	sea salt and pepper to taste	0
	Total	6

Sauté lamb in butter.
Chop scallion. Grate cheese. Combine scallion, lamb, grated cheese and couscous.
Beat egg with thyme, salt and pepper. Fold egg into couscous mixture and place in a small, greased casserole.
Set the casserole in a pan of hot water and bake for 25 minutes in an oven preheated to 350°F.
Serve hot.

Ground Steak Balls
with Goat's Cheese Centers

Good . . . Good . . . Good!

		Carbohydrates
6	ounces ground, lean sirloin steak	0
6	½-inch cubes goat's cheese	tr
¼	teaspoon ground sage	0
⅛	teaspoon sea salt	0
1	tablespoon wheat germ	2
1½	tablespoons almond kernel oil	0
	Total	2

Form the meat into 1-ounce balls with a piece of cheese in the center of each.

Mix the sage, salt and wheat germ. Roll the steak balls in the wheat germ mixture, and fry in hot oil until brown on all sides but still slightly pink in the center.

Serve immediately.

Deviled Liver and Bacon

		Carbohydrates
6	ounces calf's liver	0
1	½-inch slice slab bacon	0
4	mushrooms	4
1	tablespoon lime juice	1
2	tablespoons safflower oil	0
½	clove garlic, crushed	0
⅛	teaspoon dry mustard	0
	a generous pinch each sea salt, tarragon and chervil	0
	Total	5

Remove skin and tubes from the liver slice. Cut it into 1-inch squares.

Cut the bacon into the same size squares.

Rinse or brush the sand from the mushrooms and remove the stems.

Mix the lime juice, safflower oil, crushed garlic and spices.

Marinate the liver and mushrooms in this for 30 minutes.

Thread a 16-inch skewer with a square of liver, a square of bacon and a mushroom, and repeat until the skewer is full, ending with a mushroom.

Broil slowly about 6 inches from the flame, turning occasionally until bacon is crisp.

Serve immediately.

Beef Heart and Peppers

		Carbohydrates
2	tablespoons safflower oil	0
1	green pepper	3
4	mushrooms	1
4	thin slices beef heart	0
1	teaspoon lemon juice	tr
¼	teaspoon oregano	0
⅛	teaspoon sea salt	0
	Total	4

Heat the oil in a skillet.
Wash and dry pepper.
Remove the seeds and stem and cut into 1-inch slices.
Rinse and dry the mushrooms and cut into thick slices.
Sauté the green pepper and mushrooms for 4 minutes.
Remove the vegetables and set them aside.
Sauté the heart slices for 5 minutes, turning once.
Add the vegetables, lemon juice, oregano and sea salt.
Sauté for 5 minutes.
Serve hot.

Scallops and Shrimp en Brochette

		Carbohydrates
4	large sea scallops	9
8	shrimp	1
1½	tablespoons oil	0
1	clove garlic, crushed	0
¼	teaspoon dill weed	0
	Total	10

Rinse the scallops, cut each one into 4 pieces and drain on paper towels.

Peel the shrimp and remove the dark veins. Mix the oil, crushed garlic and dill weed. Marinate the scallop pieces and shrimp in this mixture for 30 minutes.

Thread the scallops and shrimp alternately on a skewer.

Broil approximately 6 minutes on each side or until the shellfish are thoroughly cooked and beginning to brown.

Sautéed Sea Scallops

		Carbohydrates
4	large sea scallops	9
¼	cup milk	3
1	tablespoon whole wheat flour	3
1	tablespoon butter	tr
1	tablespoon safflower oil	0
	Total	15
	Total with milk discarded	12

Rinse scallops, cut into ¾-inch slices and soak in milk for a minute or two.

Drain the slices and dip them in flour.

Heat the butter and oil to bubbling, add the scallop slices and fry to golden brown, turning once.

Serve immediately.

Tempura

I know many excellent cooks who refuse to try tempura. They are convinced that one must be Japanese by birth and have inherited all the knowledge of the East in order to master this delicate combination of tasty tidbits, cold batter and hot oil. Nonsense!

Tempura is easy to prepare. The first time you try, the results may not be perfect, but try again. You'll learn by your mistakes and soon you'll be as capable as any Japanese cook.

Carbohydrates

BATTER

2	tablespoons whole wheat flour	6
2	tablespoons rice polish	0
¼	cup ice-cold water	0
½	beaten egg	tr
⅛	teaspoon sea salt	0
	vegetable oil for deep frying (The oil may be strained and reused several times. If it becomes cloudy, simmer with an ume-boshi plum and it will clear.)	0

Total for batter   6
Batter for 1 tidbit   ½

Carbohydrates

TIDBITS *

1	slice zucchini	tr
1	slice summer squash	tr
1	shrimp	tr
1	scallop	tr
1	oyster	tr
1	2-inch piece fish fillet	0
1	sprig watercress	tr
1	cauliflower flowerette	tr
1	broccoli flowerette	tr
1	onion ring	tr

* Add the carbohydrate count of each "tidbit" plus the "batter for 1 tidbit" count.

Beat together the flour, rice polish, cold water, beaten egg and sea salt.

Shake shellfish in a bag with 2 tablespoons of flour to make sure the batter will cover completely.

Dip each tidbit in *cold* batter and drop into 3 inches of hot oil (350°F.).

Fry until golden.

Serve immediately.

Kidney and Chicken Liver Omelet

Carbohydrates

FILLING

2	lamb kidneys (3 ounces)	0
4	chicken livers	3
1½	tablespoons butter	tr
1	scallion with 3 inches green top	1
	a sprinkle each of sea salt, pepper and	
	nutmeg	0
	Total	4

OMELET

2	eggs	tr
	sea salt to taste	0
1½	tablespoons butter	tr
	Total	0
	Total for omelet with filling	4

Remove the skin and hard core from the kidneys and slice them thinly.

Cut the chicken livers into quarters. Sauté the kidneys and chicken livers in hot butter for a minute or two. Mince the scallion and add it with the spices to the pan. Stir and cook for 2 or 3 minutes more. Remove from the flame.

Beat the eggs and salt together. Melt the butter in a skillet. When the butter is hot but not brown, pour in the eggs all at one time.

Immediately begin to pull the edges of the omelet toward the center of the pan, about a half inch. As you do this, the uncooked egg will fill the vacant spaces at the sides of the pan. Repeat this until there is no more runny, uncooked egg, but the top is still very soft.

Place the filling in the center of the omelet. Tilt the handle of the pan downward toward you. One side of the omelet will slide up. Use a spatula to fold this toward the center. Now raise the handle of the pan so that the other side of the omelet slides up along the pan. Hold a plate under the pan as the omelet slides onto the dish. Tip the skillet until it is upside down and until the omelet is folded with the golden side up. If you haven't had much practice with this, and the eggs and filling get a bit jumbled, don't fret—it will taste just as delicious.

Lamb and Eggs

Here's a tasty way to use bulghour the second day.

		Carbohydrates
1	tablespoon butter	tr
½	medium onion	5
8	ounces ground lamb	0
1	hard-cooked egg	tr
1	egg	tr
2	tablespoons basic bulghour recipe	
	(see page 41)	5
⅛	teaspoon marjoram	0
⅛	teaspoon dry mustard	0
½	clove garlic, crushed	0
	sea salt and pepper to taste	0
	Total	10

Melt butter in a skillet. Chop onion and add it, with the lamb, to the butter. Sauté until the onions are golden in color.
Chop the hard-cooked egg. Beat the raw egg. Mix all ingredients.
Place in a small, buttered ovenware dish and bake for 45 minutes in an oven preheated to 350°F.
Serve hot.

Sprout and Spinach Scrambled Eggs

		Carbohydrates
1	cup fresh spinach, loosely packed	7
¼	cup adzuki bean (or other) sprouts	1
1	teaspoon butter	tr
2	eggs	tr
1	1-inch cube goat's cheese, grated	tr
	a pinch of fresh or dried basil	0
	sea salt to taste	0
	Total	8

Wash the spinach and clip the beans from the sprouts.
Melt the butter in a skillet and add the spinach with the water remaining on the leaves.
Cover, steam for 2 minutes, and cut into shreds.
Add all ingredients to pan and stir until the eggs are as you like them.
Serve immediately.

Fried Eggs with Tomato and Alfalfa Sprouts

		Carbohydrates
1	tablespoon butter	tr
2	slices tomato	0
2	eggs	tr
2	tablespoons alfalfa sprouts	0
	sea salt and pepper to taste	0
	Total	tr

Melt butter in skillet. Sauté the tomato slices for a minute or so, turning once. Remove tomato slices from pan and set aside. Break the eggs in the butter in the skillet. Add more butter if necessary.

Cover and cook over low heat for 5 minutes or until the eggs are nearly set on the top.

Arrange the tomato slices alongside the eggs, and place the pan under the broiler for a minute or two (longer if you like the yolks firm).

Remove the pan from the broiler and slide the eggs and tomato slices onto a serving plate, taking care not to break the yolks. Top the tomato with the sprouts. Sprinkle the eggs with sea salt and pepper.

Serve hot.

Egg and Cheese Casserole

		Carbohydrates
1	scallion with 3 inches green top	1
1	1-inch cube cheese	tr
2	tablespoons leftover cooked bulghour (page 41)	5
1	egg	tr
	sea salt and pepper to taste	0
	Total	6

Chop scallion. Grate cheese. Combine scallion, grated cheese and bulghour.

Beat egg, salt and pepper.

Fold egg into bulghour mixture and place in a small, greased casserole.

Set the casserole in a pan of hot water and bake for 25 minutes in an oven preheated to 350°F.

Serve hot.

Fried Stuffed Eggs

		Carbohydrates
2	hard-cooked eggs	tr
3	large mushrooms	4½
½	clove garlic	0
¼	teaspoon finely chopped dulse	0
1	tablespoon butter	tr
2	teaspoons heavy cream	tr
	a pinch each of pepper and nutmeg	0
1	raw egg, beaten	tr
1	teaspoon wheat germ	½
2	teaspoons whole wheat bread crumbs	1
	safflower oil for frying	0
4	sprigs watercress	tr
	Total	6
	Total for 1	1½

Split hard-cooked eggs lengthwise.

Remove yolks and press them through a fine sieve.

Grind together the mushrooms, garlic and dulse.

Melt the butter in a saucepan and stir in the mushroom mixture. Cook for 2 minutes, stirring constantly. Add half the sieved egg yolk, the heavy cream and the spices. Mix well.

Fill the egg whites with this mixture and round out to resemble a whole egg.

Dip the stuffed eggs in the beaten egg and then roll them in the wheat germ–bread crumb mixture.

Chill for at least 1 hour. Fry until golden brown in a basket, in hot fat.

Serve hot on a plate of watercress sprigs topped with the remaining sieved egg yolk.

Baked Artichoke with Egg Filling

		Carbohydrates
1	small artichoke	5½
2	cups water	0
1	tablespoon basic bulghour recipe (see page 41)	2½
2	tablespoons grated cheese	tr
1	egg	tr
1	scallion, minced	1
	Total	9

Steam artichoke in water in a covered glass pot until tender, about 45 minutes.

Meanwhile mix the bulghour, grated cheese, egg and scallion. Drain the artichoke, remove several of the center leaves and pull out the choke.

Fill with the egg mixture and place in an ovenproof dish.

Bake for 45 minutes in an oven preheated to 400°F.

Serve hot.

vegetables

Low Calorie Vegetables

Spicy Cauliflower with Yoghurt

This is cauliflower with an Eastern accent.

		Calories
2	cups uncooked cauliflower flowerettes (cooks down to 1½ cups)	50
⅛	teaspoon each curry powder, chili powder, powdered saffron	0
¼	teaspoon sea salt	0
¼	cup water	0
2	tablespoons yoghurt	16
	a sprinkle of paprika	0
	Total	66

Place in a skillet and sprinkle with spices and sea salt.
Add water, cover and steam over low heat until cauliflower is tender but still slightly crisp.
Top with cold yoghurt, sprinkle with paprika and serve.

Cauliflower and Cabbage

		Calories
1	tablespoon safflower oil	125
1	teaspoon mustard seeds	0
1	teaspoon sesame seeds	13
⅛	teaspoon each powdered cinnamon, cloves and cumin	0
⅛	small head cabbage	15
1	cup cauliflower flowerettes	14
¼	teaspoon sea salt	0
1	tablespoon yoghurt	8
	Total	175

Heat the oil in a skillet. Add mustard seeds, sesame seeds, cinnamon, cloves and cumin. Stir over medium heat for 1 minute. Trim hard core and limp outer leaves from the cabbage and discard; cut the vegetable into long shreds.
Add the cauliflower, cabbage and salt to the skillet and stir-fry for 5 minutes. Stir in yoghurt and simmer for 3 minutes.
Serve hot.

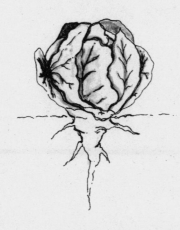

Japanese Cabbage

		Calories
⅛	head white cabbage	15
¼	cup water	0
	a dash of sea salt	0
2	teaspoons white miso	16
2	teaspoons organic raw sugar	34
2	teaspoons vinegar	1
¼	teaspoon dry mustard	0
½	teaspoon black sesame seeds	6
	Total	72

Use a large knife to shred the cabbage.
Place cabbage, water and salt in a heavy pot. Cover and cook over medium heat for 8–10 minutes.
Drain cabbage well.
Mix miso, sugar, vinegar and mustard, and stir into the hot cabbage.
Sprinkle with sesame seeds.
Serve hot.

Broiled Sweet Potato

		Calories
1	sweet potato	155
¼	teaspoon almond kernel oil	10
	Total	165
	Total without skin	96

Wash sweet potato and cut in half lengthwise.
Make 3 deep gashes in the cut side of each half.
Rub all sides with oil.
Place on low rack of broiler. Turn frequently.
If skin browns too much, lower broiler flame. Broil until soft or about 35 minutes.
Serve hot.

Carrots with Sour Cream Sauce

		Calories
1	large carrot (or 2 small ones)	30
1	teaspoon butter	33
⅛	teaspoon thyme	0
	sea salt and pepper to taste	0
2	teaspoons sour cream	20
1	teaspoon milk	3
	Total	86

Wash carrot and cut it into long, thin strips.
Melt the butter in a Teflon pan and sauté the carrot strips for 8 minutes or until they are still slightly crispy. Sprinkle with thyme, salt and pepper, and remove pan from the heat.
Stir in the sour cream and the milk and reheat.
Serve hot.

Carrot Slices in Orange Sauce

		Calories
2	medium-sized carrots	40
½	cup orange juice	56
1	teaspoon honey	22
	a pinch of nutmeg	0
	Total	118

Wash carrots and remove tops. Cut the vegetables into ¼-inch slices and place them in a skillet. Add the orange juice, honey and nutmeg, and simmer, covered, until barely tender. Serve hot.

Baked Acorn Squash

You don't have to be on a diet to enjoy lovely, golden baked squash with honey.

		Calories
½	acorn squash	58
	several tablespoons water	0
2	teaspoons honey	44
	a pinch of nutmeg and cloves	0
	Total	102

Cut squash in half and scoop out seeds.
Cut a thin slice from the bottom of each half to keep it from tipping.
Fill hollow with water, honey, nutmeg and cloves.
Place on a baking sheet and bake for 1 hour at 350°F. until tender.
Serve hot.

Steamed Sweet Potato Slices
with Apple

High in calories, but good for a change. This doubles and quadruples nicely.

		Calories
½	medium-sized sweet potato	77
½	teaspoon butter	17
2	tablespoons water	0
⅛	teaspoon sea salt	0
	a sprinkle of nutmeg	0
1	medium-sized McIntosh apple	70
	Total	164

Peel ½ sweet potato and cut into ¼-inch slices.
Melt butter in a Teflon skillet. Toss the potato slices to coat them with butter. Cook over low heat for a few minutes and turn them.
Add the water, salt and nutmeg, and steam the potatoes until they are fairly soft.
Core the apple and cut it in ½-inch slices.
Arrange these in a spiral design on top of the potatoes and cook for a minute or two, adding a bit more water if necessary to keep the potatoes from scorching.
Serve hot.

Healthy Pennsylvania Dutch Tomatoes

My grandmother fried tomatoes this way over 30 years ago. The sprouts are my addition.

		Calories
2	small or 1 large tomato	50
1	teaspoon whole wheat flour	5
1	teaspoon wheat germ	5
2	teaspoons butter	66
1	teaspoon organic raw sugar	17
2	tablespoons milk	20
1	tablespoon alfalfa sprouts	1
	Total	164

Slice tomatoes.

Mix flour and wheat germ. Coat tomato slices in this, and sauté in butter in a Teflon pan for a few minutes. Sprinkle with sugar and turn tomato slices. Fry until brown, add milk and cook 1 minute more.

Place tomato slices on plate and top with sauce from pan and alfalfa sprouts.

Serve immediately.

Sweet and Sour Apple–Cabbage

		Calories
¼	head red cabbage	30
1	small onion	30
1	apple	70
1	cup water	0
¼	teaspoon sea salt	0
1	tablespoon honey	66
1	teaspoon lemon juice	1
	Total	197

Remove the hard core and the limp outer leaves of the cabbage.
Grate the cabbage, the onion and the apple.
Place all ingredients in a skillet, cover and simmer for 30 minutes, adding more water if necessary.
Serve hot.

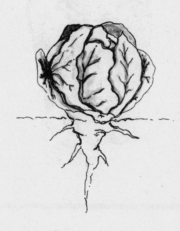

Sweet and Salty Corn

		Calories
1	ear corn	70
1	tablespoon honey	66
1½	teaspoons sea salt	0
	Total	136
	Total with honey and water poured off	75

Husk the corn and remove the silk.
Place in a small pan or skillet with just enough water to cover.
Add the honey and sea salt, and cook over medium heat for 10 minutes.
Reduce the remaining liquid by half.
Dip the corn in this and serve immediately.

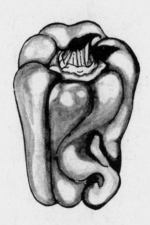

Stuffed Green Peppers

		Calories
2	small green peppers	20
1	slice whole grain bread	60
3	tablespoons basic beef stock (see page 39)	21
2	carrots	40
1	stalk celery	5
1	tablespoon chopped raw cashew nuts	47
1	tablespoon yoghurt	8
2	tablespoons basic bulghour recipe (see page 41)	26
1	tablespoon pine nuts	80
1	tablespoon raisins	35
¼	teaspoon thyme	0
¼	teaspoon salt	0
	Total	342

Cut the tops from the green peppers and set them aside.
Remove pith and seeds from the peppers, rinse them and turn them upside down to drain.
Crumble the bread and soften it in the beef stock. Chop the carrots, celery and cashew nuts and place them with the yoghurt in the container of your blender. Blend until smooth, turning off the blender several times to push the vegetables down against the blades.
Mix all ingredients except the green peppers.
Stuff the peppers with this filling, replace the tops, and place them in a covered dish to which you have added ¼ inch of water. Bake at 375°F for 20 minutes.

Eggplant with Miso

This stores well and is delicious cold or served as an hors d'oeuvre. If you don't feel like making Eggplant Pickles, why not make a double portion of this recipe and feast tomorrow as well as today.

		Calories
½	eggplant	22
1	tablespoon almond kernel oil	125
4	scallions	16
1	tablespoon red miso	· 24
1	tablespoon organic raw sugar	51
2	tablespoons water	0
1	teaspoon vinegar	1
	Total	239

Cut eggplant into ¾-inch cubes. Heat oil in a Teflon skillet and stir in the eggplant. Lower heat to medium and cook for 5 minutes, stirring occasionally.
Chop scallions. Mix miso, sugar, water and vinegar, and pour over the eggplant.
Stir over low heat for 3–4 minutes. Add scallions and stir for 1 minute more.
Serve hot either alone or with a few tablespoons of brown rice.

String Beans Biscay

Hard-cooked egg slices and ripe olives lend flavor to this unusual recipe.

		Calories
2	teaspoons butter	66
1	small onion	30
½	medium-sized green pepper	7
½	clove garlic	0
½	medium-sized tomato, chopped	17
¼	cup chicken stock (page 37)	0
20	whole string beans	28
	a generous pinch each of thyme and	
	cayenne pepper	0
1	hard-cooked egg, sliced	75
1	teaspoon capers	1
4	pitted black olives, sliced	30
	Total	254

Melt butter in Teflon skillet. Peel and slice onion and separate slices into rings.

Remove stem and seeds from green pepper and chop. Sauté onion and green pepper until the onion turns golden. Add garlic and chopped tomato and simmer for 5 minutes.

Add chicken stock, string beans and spices.

Cover and simmer for 15–20 minutes.

Remove cover and cook for 5 minutes more or until beans are barely tender and most of the liquid has disappeared.

Serve hot, decorated with hard-cooked egg slices, capers and sliced olives.

Okra-Stuffed Pepper

		Calories
1	medium-sized green pepper	15
¼	cup chopped onion	16
1	teaspoon safflower oil	42
¼	cup brown-bread crumbs	52
½	small tomato	12
½	cup sliced, fresh okra	12
⅛	teaspoon sea salt	0
	Total	149

Cut the top from the pepper and remove the seeds.
Cook for 5 minutes in boiling water. Drain.
Sauté onion in hot oil for 3 minutes. Add the bread crumbs and stir over medium heat for 2 minutes more.
Add the remaining ingredients and cook until the mixture is quite thick.
Fill the pepper with the okra stuffing, place in an oiled baking dish and bake for 25 minutes in an oven preheated to 350°F. Serve hot or cold.

Low Carbohydrate Vegetables

Fried Spinach with Cheese

Even if you hate spinach you'll love this!

		Carbohydrates
2	cups spinach	6
1	small egg	tr
1	tablespoon wheat germ	2
	a sprinkle each sea salt, pepper and nutmeg	0
1	tablespoon butter	tr
2	tablespoons grated goat's cheese	tr
	Total	8

Wash spinach leaves (no stems) and place them in an enamel pan with only the water clinging to them. Cover the pan and cook over low heat until the spinach is wilted. Pour the liquid from the pan into your jar of vegetable stock.
Use two knives to shred the spinach.
Beat in the egg, wheat germ and spices.
Melt the butter in a small skillet. Pour in the spinach mixture and fry over medium heat for 3 minutes or until the bottom is brown. Turn and sprinkle with grated cheese.
Fry for a few minutes and serve hot.

Spinach with Egg–Cheese Topping

Spinach never tasted better than this, served under a rich egg yolk and cheese topping.

		Carbohydrates
¼	teaspoon safflower oil	0
1	cup cooked leftover spinach	6
⅛	teaspoon sea salt	0
	a pinch of nutmeg	0
1	tablespoon butter	tr
2	egg yolks	tr
1	1-inch cube goat's cheese, grated	tr
1	tablespoon heavy cream	tr
	Total	6

Grease individual ovenproof baking dish and add spinach.
Sprinkle with sea salt and nutmeg.
Melt butter in a small pan, remove from heat and stir in egg yolks, grated cheese and heavy cream, all at once.
Top the spinach with this and heat for 10 minutes in an oven preheated to 325°F.

Green Beans with Mustard Sauce

These beans are HOT! But oh, so good!

		Carbohydrates
1	cup green beans	6
½	tablespoon butter	tr
¼	teaspoon dry mustard	0
1	egg yolk	tr
1	tablespoon milk	1
½	teaspoon vinegar	0
½	teaspoon wheat germ	tr
1	tablespoon mustard sprouts	0
	Total	7

Wash the beans, snap them and discard their stems. Steam in a small amount of water until beans are tender. Pour any remaining liquid into your vegetable stock jar.

Melt the butter in the same pan in which you cooked the beans. Mix the dry mustard, egg yolk and milk in a bowl. Remove the beans from the flame and spoon them into the egg yolk mixture.

Pour the beans and sauce back into the pan and stir over very low heat until the sauce thickens slightly.

Add the vinegar, stir once more, and place the mustard-coated beans on a serving plate. Sprinkle with wheat germ and top with crisp sprouts.

Serve immediately.

Green Beans with Sprouts

		Carbohydrates
1½	cups green beans	9
1	strip bacon	½
¼	medium-sized tomato, diced	9
	a pinch each curry and chili powders	0
½	clove garlic	0
4	tablespoons water	0
1	tablespoon alfalfa sprouts	0
	Total	18½

Wash the beans, drain them and cut them into thin, diagonal slices, discarding stems.
Cut bacon into fine dice and fry over medium heat until crisp.
Sauté the beans in the bacon fat for 5 minutes.
Add the tomato, curry, chili powder, garlic and water, and cook over low flame for 15 minutes or until beans are tender.
Discard garlic, top with sprouts and serve immediately.

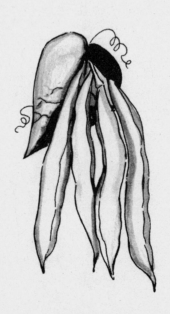

Broccoli Baked with Cheese

		Carbohydrates
1	cup broccoli spears	7
2	tablespoons butter	tr
1	egg yolk	tr
3	tablespoons milk	2
1	1-inch square goat's cheese, grated	tr
	a pinch each of nutmeg, sea salt and pepper	0
	Total	9

Wash the broccoli, discarding the large leaves and tough lower stalks.

Split the tops, cover and cook until tender in butter, over a very low flame.

Arrange the stalks in a baking dish. Mix the egg yolk and milk and pour this over the broccoli. Top with grated cheese and spices and any melted butter remaining in the pan.

Bake for 20 minutes in an oven preheated to 350°F.

Serve immediately.

To serve 4: Double quantities of butter and cheese and multiply all other ingredients by 4. Bake for 35 minutes in an oven pre-heated to 350°F.

Broccoli Amandine

		Carbohydrates
1	cup chopped broccoli	7
2	scallions with 3 inches green top	2
⅛	cup blanched almonds	3½
1½	tablespoons butter	tr
	Total	12½

Chop scallions.
Cut nuts into slivers.
Melt butter in skillet. Add all ingredients.
Stir-fry until broccoli is tender but still a bit crunchy.
Serve hot.

Zucchini with Basil

Good tastes from the earth, cooked simply so as not to disguise the natural flavor.

		Carbohydrates
1	small zucchini	6
2	teaspoons butter	tr
1	tablespoon chopped parsley	0
1	tablespoon chopped fresh basil	0
	Total	6

Rub zucchini with rough cloth, rinse in cool water and cut into ¼-inch slices.
Melt butter in Teflon pan and sauté zucchini for 5 minutes or until barely tender. Add chopped parsley and basil and stir over low heat for 1 minute.
Serve hot.

Zucchini-Stuffed Summer Squash

Prepare this recipe today, and for tomorrow do a turnabout and stuff the zucchini with summer squash. Both are delicious!

		Carbohydrates
½	small (8-ounce) summer squash	4
½	zucchini	3
1½	tablespoons butter	tr
½	clove garlic, crushed	0
1	tablespoon brown-bread crumbs	2
	sea salt to taste	0
	Total	9

Wash the summer squash and the zucchini with a rough cloth and split lengthwise.
Scoop out the summer squash and chop the center pieces.
Chop the zucchini.
Sauté garlic and bread crumbs in butter for 2 minutes.
Add the chopped summer squash, zucchini and salt.
Stir over medium heat for 5 minutes.
Rub the half summer squash with oil and fill.
Bake for 45 minutes in an oven preheated to 300°F.

Zucchini with Sweet and Sour Dill Sauce

		Carbohydrates
1	zucchini (about 6 ounces)	6
2	teaspoons butter	tr
1	teaspoon chopped fresh dill (or ½ teaspoon dried dill weed)	0
	sea salt to taste	0
2	tablespoons sour cream	1
½	teaspoon lemon juice	tr
½	teaspoon organic raw sugar	0
	a dash of paprika	0
	Total	7

Wash the zucchini with a rough cloth and cut into ¼-inch slices.

Sauté in butter with dill and salt over low heat until the zucchini is barely tender. Do not overcook.

Mix the sour cream, lemon juice and sugar, and stir this into the zucchini slices. Heat over very low flame for 1 minute, stirring constantly.

Serve immediately, sprinkled with paprika.

Swedish Cabbage

		Carbohydrates
¼	head small cabbage	6
¾	cup water	0
¼	teaspoon sea salt	0
2	tablespoons sour cream	1
¼	teaspoon caraway seeds	0
	Total	7

Shred the cabbage and cook it, covered, in salted water until tender.
Drain off any liquid, add the sour cream and caraway seeds and stir over a very low flame for 2 minutes.
Serve hot.

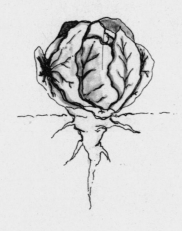

Curried Cabbage au Gratin

This doubles and quadruples nicely. Allow ½ cabbage for every 3 persons.

		Carbohydrates
¼	small head cabbage	6
1	cup beef stock	6
1	bay leaf	0
½	garlic clove, crushed	0
	a pinch of powdered cloves	0
½	teaspoon curry powder	0
3	tablespoons heavy cream	tr
1	1-inch cube cheese, grated	tr
1	teaspoon wheat germ	½
	Total	12½

Remove the hard core and the limp outer leaves of the cabbage. Shred the cabbage and place it, along with the beef stock, bay leaf, crushed garlic, cloves and curry powder, in a skillet. Cover and cook until tender. Drain the remaining stock into your beef stock jar.

Add the heavy cream to the drained cabbage and cook over high heat for 1 minute.

Place the cabbage in a buttered ovenproof dish, sprinkle with grated cheese and wheat germ and bake for 15 minutes in an oven preheated to 350°F.

Serve hot.

Endive with Soy Sauce

		Carbohydrates
½	endive (3 ounces)	3
1	tablespoon safflower oil	0
1	teaspoon soy sauce	0
	sea salt to taste	0
	Total	3

Cut endive in half lengthwise. Fry very quickly in piping hot oil.
Sprinkle with soy sauce and salt.
Serve immediately.

Fried Acorn Squash

Extra filling and super-nutritious, acorn squash is one of the
nice things about winter.

		Carbohydrates
½	small acorn squash	16
1½	tablespoons safflower oil	0
⅛	teaspoon each nutmeg and sea salt	0
	Total	16

Remove the seeds and peel and slice acorn squash.
Fry in hot oil until each slice is golden brown on both sides.
Sprinkle with nutmeg and salt.
Serve hot.

salads

Low Calorie Salads

Sprout Salad

Almost any variation of salad greens may be used.

		Calories
2	large lettuce leaves	10
½	cup watercress leaves without tough stems	2
1	small tomato	25
1	tablespoon vinegar	2
2	teaspoons honey	44
	sea salt and pepper to taste	0
¼	cup sprouts	4
	Total	87

Wash and shred lettuce. Wash watercress and pick off the leaves.
Wash and chop tomato. Mix vinegar, honey, sea salt and pepper.
Toss all ingredients together.
Serve cold.

Cucumber Salad

This is so good you might want to prepare a double portion and hide some away for tomorrow's lunch.

		Calories
½	medium-sized cucumber	15
1	tablespoon tarragon vinegar	2
2	teaspoons organic raw sugar	34
2	tablespoons water	0
	sea salt and pepper to taste	0
1	teaspoon yoghurt	3
	a pinch of tarragon leaves	0
	Total	54

Cut cucumber into very thin slices and place evenly on a large plate.
Top with paper towels, cover with a heavy plate and place in the refrigerator for 20 minutes. Meanwhile, bring to a boil vinegar, sugar, water, salt and pepper. Mix cucumber slices and vinegar mixture and refrigerate until thoroughly chilled. Top with yoghurt and tarragon leaves and serve cold.

Raw Cucumber Stuffed with Crabmeat

Makes approximately 10 slices

Serve this as a luncheon salad or as a low calorie snack or appetizer.

		Calories
1	cucumber	30
1	scallion with 2 inches green top	4
2	ounces cooked crabmeat	60
1	teaspoon vinegar	1
½	teaspoon organic raw sugar	8
½	teaspoon soy sauce	1
	Total	104
	Total for 1 slice	10

Peel the cucumber and cut 1 inch from one end.
Scoop out the cucumber seeds.
Cut the root from the scallion and mince the scallion and the crabmeat.
Stir the vinegar, sugar, soy sauce, crabmeat and scallion together and stuff the cucumber with this mixture.
Refrigerate for 1 hour or longer.
Cut into ½-inch slices and serve cold as a salad or as an accompaniment to Sushi, (page 44).

Nasturtium Salad

The leaf of the nasturtium has a rather peppery, distinctive taste . . . and the flowers are good, too.

		Calories
¼	head lettuce	13
1	tablespoon yoghurt mayonnaise (see page 33)	19
1	tablespoon chopped fresh nasturtium leaves	0
3	nasturtium flowers	0
	Total	32

Place lettuce on salad plate.
Top with yoghurt mayonnaise, chopped nasturtium leaves and nasturtium flowers.
Serve immediately.

Bulghour Health Salad

Here's a salad that's a little different—and more nutritious than most. Practically a meal in itself.

		Calories
¼	large green pepper	6
¼	large cucumber	7
½	medium-sized tomato	17
1	scallion with 3 inches green top	4
2	tablespoons cold basic bulghour recipe (see page 41)	26
2	teaspoons ketchup	30
1	tablespoon lemon juice	5
	a pinch or two of cayenne pepper	0
	sea salt to taste	0
2	teaspoons wheat germ	10
	Total	105

Wash vegetables and finely dice them.
Mix diced vegetables and remaining ingredients.

Pinto Bean Salad

Serves 2

This salad doubles as an appetizer.

		Calories
½	cup cooked pinto beans	279
½	small onion, chopped	4
3	tablespoons chopped winter wheat sprouts	3
1	tablespoon chopped parsley	1
2	teaspoons lemon juice	2
2	teaspoons safflower oil	84
⅛	teaspoon sea salt	0
⅛	teaspoon oregano	0
	Total	373
	Total for 1	186

Mix ½ cup pinto beans cooked until tender, cooled and drained, with all other ingredients.
Chill.
Serve cold on a lettuce leaf.

Cold Broccoli Salad

		Calories
1	cup broccoli spears	45
1	teaspoon olive oil	42
1	teaspoon lemon juice	1
½	clove garlic, crushed	0
½	teaspoon minced chervil	0
1	tablespoon yoghurt	8
	Total	96

Wash the broccoli, discarding the large leaves and tough lower stalks.
Split the tops and cook until tender in water to cover.
Drain the broccoli and add the liquid to your jar of vegetable stock.
Toss the cooked broccoli in olive oil and lemon juice that has been mixed with crushed garlic clove and minced chervil.
Refrigerate for at least 1 hour.
Serve cold topped with yoghurt.

Jellied Carrot "Salmon" Salad

This cool salad tastes like salmon but has far fewer calories and many more vitamins.

		Calories
3	medium-sized carrots	60
¼	cup raw cashew nuts	190
½	tablespoon peanut butter	47
1	tablespoon yoghurt	8
2	teaspoons water	0
⅛	teaspoon sea salt	0
¼	teaspoon dill weed	0
1	teaspoon unflavored gelatin	3
3	tablespoons water	0
¼	teaspoon lemon juice	0
	Total	308

Wash the carrots and remove the stems and roots.

Chop the vegetables and the cashew nuts and place them, along with the peanut butter, yoghurt, 2 teaspoons of water, salt and dill, in the container of your blender.

Blend until fairly smooth, turning off the blender several times to push down the carrots.

Soften the gelatin in 3 tablespoons of water, add the lemon juice and heat over a very low flame until the gelatin is dissolved.

Stir the carrot mixture into the gelatin, place in a small salmon mold or fluted mold and refrigerate for 2 hours.

To serve, wrap a hot towel around the mold to loosen the "salmon" and turn onto a small plate of shredded lettuce.

Apple Salad

		Calories
1	apple	70
½	cup watercress	2
1	teaspoon almond kernel oil	42
1	teaspoon vinegar	1
¼	teaspoon organic raw sugar	4
	sea salt and pepper to taste	0
¼	teaspoon minced, fresh or dried chervil	0
1	tablespoon dried wheat-bread crumbs	13
	Total	132

Core the apple and thinly slice.

Wash the watercress, remove any thick stems and blot on paper towels.

Mix the oil, vinegar, sugar, salt, pepper and chervil.

Toss this dressing with the apple and watercress and top the salad with wheat crumbs.

Serve cold.

Apple Cole Slaw

This interesting concoction not only tastes terrific, but it's awfully good for you!

		Calories
⅛	head of cabbage	15
½	apple	35
¼	cup milk	40
2	tablespoons tarragon vinegar	4
1	tablespoon organic raw sugar	51
⅛	teaspoon sea salt	0
1	tablespoon cottage cheese	12
¼	cup bean sprouts	4
	Total	161

Cut the core from the cabbage and the apple. Use a large knife to cut cabbage into thin shreds.

Cut the apple into ⅛-inch slices. Place apple slices on top of the shredded cabbage and chop both fine.

Blend milk, vinegar, sugar, salt and cottage cheese. Mix this dressing with the shredded cabbage, apple and bean sprouts. Serve cold.

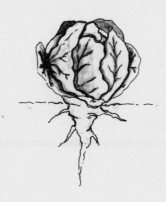

Banana Cole Slaw

		Calories
¼	small head cabbage	30
½	banana	42
1	tablespoon honey	66
¼	cup plain yoghurt	30
1	tablespoon sunflower kernels	21
	Total	189

Remove hard center core and shred cabbage.
Slice banana.
Mix all ingredients.
Serve cold.

Avocado–Bean Curd Salad

		Calories
½	cup bean curd, cut in cubes (see page 43)	80
¼	avocado, cut in cubes	92
1	small carrot	20
1	cup fresh spinach, loosely packed	44
2	tablespoons sunflower seed kernels	42
1	tablespoon lemon juice	5
2	tablespoons soy sauce	20
	a generous pinch of marjoram	0
	Total	303

Place bean curd and avocado in salad bowl.
Rinse carrot and slice thinly.
Toss all ingredients.
Serve cold.

Zucchini Salad

Zucchini may be even more tasty cold than it is hot . . .

		Calories
1	zucchini (about 6 ounces)	6
2	teaspoons saffower oil	84
2	teaspoons tarragon vinegar	1
	sea salt to taste	0
1	teaspoon organic raw sugar	17
1	teaspoon chopped fresh basil	0
	Total	108

Wash zucchini with a rough cloth and cut into ¼-inch slices.
Heat the oil in a skillet and sauté zucchini over medium heat
for 3 minutes, stirring constantly.
Drain and chill the zucchini. Add the vinegar, salt and sugar to
the pan, bring the mixture to a boil and then cool to room
temperature.
Stir in the basil and chilled zucchini.

Asparagus with Sesame Seeds

		Calories
1	cup asparagus spears, diagonally cut	35
½	teaspoon safflower oil	21
½	teaspoon white sesame seeds	6
1	teaspoon vinegar	1
½	teaspoon organic raw sugar	8
½	teaspoon soy sauce	1
	Total	72

Steam the asparagus and set aside.
Heat the oil in a skillet and lightly brown the sesame seeds.
Mix all ingredients and refrigerate.
Serve cold.

Orange and Watercress Salad

		Calories
1	cup watercress	4
½	small orange	30
3	scallions including 2 inches green top	12
1	teaspoon safflower oil	42
2	teaspoons cider vinegar	1
	Total	89

Wash watercress very thoroughly. It tends to harbor snails, and these, while friendly, do not encourage the appetite.
Peel orange and cut into thin slices. Chop scallions. Mix oil and vinegar. Toss all ingredients in a salad bowl.
Serve immediately.

Low Carbohydrate Salads

Stuffed Endive

		Carbohydrates
1	endive	2
2	tablespoons cream cheese	tr
½	tablespoon chopped chives	tr
¼	teaspoon curry powder	0
⅛	teaspoon sea salt	0
1	tablespoon chopped winter wheat sprouts	0
8	walnut halves	2
	Total	4
	Total for 1 half	2

Trim the endive and cut it in half lengthwise.
Mix the cream cheese, chives, curry powder and salt.
Use a pastry tube to pipe one-half of this mixture down the center of each endive half. Sprinkle with wheat sprouts.
Arrange the walnuts attractively on the cheese filling.
Refrigerate.
Serve cold.

Summer Salad

Here's a lunch in a bowl or a salad to serve with a plain meat meal.

		Carbohydrates
½	cucumber	3
2	scallions with 3 inches green top	2
½	medium-sized tomato	3
½	small green pepper	1
2	teaspoons lime or lemon juice	tr
2	teaspoons safflower oil	0
1	teaspoon minced fresh mint	tr
½	teaspoon wheat germ	tr
	Total	9

Finely chop cucumber, scallions, tomato and green pepper and toss with lime juice, oil and mint.
Chill.
Sprinkle with wheat germ and serve immediately.

Spinach and Tarragon Salad

		Carbohydrates
¼	cup fresh spinach	2
¼	cup parsley	tr
6	tarragon leaves, finely chopped	0
¼	cup thinly sliced zucchini	2
1	tablespoon safflower oil	0
1½	teaspoons lime juice	½
⅛	teaspoon sea salt	0
½	clove garlic, crushed	0
	Total	4½

Wash vegetables and drain on paper towels.
Toss all ingredients together.
Serve immediately.

Brain Salad

		Carbohydrates
3½	ounces cooked brains (beef, calf or sheep)	0
½	cucumber	4
1	scallion with 1 inch green top	1
1	tablespoon water	0
¼	teaspoon dry mustard	0
1	teaspoon vinegar	tr
½	teaspoon organic raw sugar	0
	Total	5

Remove black veins and membranes from the brains and cut them into cubes.

Cut cucumber lengthwise and remove the seeds. Slice the cucumber thinly, crosswise.

Trim the scallion and mince it.

Mix the water, mustard, vinegar, sugar, sliced cucumber and minced scallion.

Pour over the brains, and marinate for at least 1 hour.

Serve cold.

Lettuce with Hard-Cooked Egg Dressing

		Carbohydrates
1	hard-cooked egg	tr
1	tablespoon yoghurt	1
1	tablespoon mayonnaise	0
1	scallion	1
¼	head lettuce	3
	a sprinkle of paprika	0
	Total	5

Chop egg and mix with yoghurt, mayonnaise and minced scallion. Top lettuce with yoghurt–egg mixture, sprinkle with paprika and serve cold.

Sweet and Sour Cabbage
with Poppy Seeds

Here is a vegetable that tastes like a salad—or vice versa—and may be served as either one.

		Carbohydrates
⅛	head cabbage	3
¼	cup water	0
2½	tablespoons vinegar	2½
1	tablespoon honey	17
1	tablespoon water	0
⅛	teaspoon sea salt	0
¼	teaspoon poppy seeds	0
	Total	22½

Use a large knife to shred the cabbage. Place cabbage and ¼ cup of water in a heavy pot. Cover and cook over medium heat for 8–10 minutes.
Cabbage should be fairly crisp.
Drain cabbage and blot with paper towels.
Bring vinegar, honey, 1 tablespoon of water and sea salt to a boil in a medium-sized skillet. Stir in cabbage and continue to cook for 1 minute.
Sprinkle with poppy seeds.
Serve hot or cold.

Hot Cucumber Salad

		Carbohydrates
3	slices bacon	1½
½	large cucumber	7
½	teaspoon dry mustard	0
1	teaspoon water	0
1	tablespoon vinegar	2
1	teaspoon organic raw sugar	1
	Total	11½

Dice bacon and fry over medium heat until well done but not brown.

Cut cucumber into paper-thin slices.

Make a paste of the mustard, water, vinegar and sugar.

Place the cucumber slices in the pan, add the mustard paste and stir over medium heat for 1 minute.

Serve immediately.

Mushroom Salad

		Carbohydrates
4	medium-sized mushrooms	4
2	tablespoons vinegar	2
¼	cup safflower oil	0
1	large lettuce leaf	1
2	tablespoons alfalfa sprouts	0
½	hard-cooked egg, sliced	tr
1	tablespoon shredded green pepper	tr
	sea salt and pepper to taste	0
	Total	7
	Total with marinade discarded	6

Rinse mushrooms and cut into thin slices.

Mix vinegar and oil and marinate the mushroom slices in the refrigerator for at least 1 hour.

Wash, drain and chill the lettuce leaf.

To serve, place the lettuce on a salad plate, top with the drained mushroom slices, alfalfa sprouts, hard-cooked egg slices, shredded green pepper, salt and pepper in that order. Serve cold.

desserts

Low Calorie Desserts

Cran–Apple Sherbet

Serves 3

Here's a festive dessert good enough to turn any day into a holiday.

		Calories
1	cup whole cranberries	100
1	large Delicious apple	70
3	tablespoons raw buckwheat honey	198
2	tablespoons plain yoghurt	16
	Total	384
	Total for 1 portion	128

Wash and pick over cranberries, discarding stems and soft berries.

Peel and core apple and cut it into ½-inch cubes.

Place honey, apple and cranberries in blender container and purée.

Pour cranberry–apple purée into refrigerator tray, stir in yoghurt.

Freeze until mushy, stir and continue freezing.

Strawberry Yoghurt Sherbet

Serves 3

		Calories
1	cup yoghurt	120
1	cup fresh, ripe strawberries	55
2	tablespoons honey	132
	Total	307
	Total for 1 portion	102

Freeze the yoghurt in a refrigerator tray.
Purée the strawberries and honey in the container of your blender.
Beat the frozen yoghurt into the strawberry purée and place in refrigerator tray.
Freeze.

Frozen Strawberry Cream

2 portions

Excellent with a fruit salad or as a creamy dessert.

		Calories
1	cup whole, ripe strawberries	55
2	tablespoons honey	132
¾	cup cottage cheese	137
	Total	324
	Total for 1	162

Place all ingredients in the container of your blender. Blend on low speed until smooth.
Divide equally in two small glass dishes.
Freeze until mushy and stir with a fork. Refreeze.
Remove from freezer a few moments before serving.

Frozen Prune Whip

Makes 4 small portions

Try freezing this in fancy individual molds.

		Calories
8	dried, pitted prunes	140
½	cup water	0
½	apple, cored	35
3	tablespoons cottage cheese	36
2	tablespoons honey	132
2	tablespoons yoghurt	16
⅛	teaspoon cinnamon	0
	Total	359
	Total for 1 portion	90

Soak the prunes in the water for 1 hour. Simmer them in the same water until the prunes are tender and there are about 2 tablespoons of syrup in the bottom of the pot.

Place the prunes and syrup in the container of your blender. Chop the apple and add it, with the cottage cheese and honey, to the blender container. Blend on high speed for 5 minutes, stopping the blender occasionally to push the fruit down against the blades.

Gently stir the yoghurt and cinnamon into the prune mixture. Place in a bowl and freeze until mushy.

Beat the prune whip with a fork until it is fluffy.

Spoon into individual molds and refreeze.

Remove from freezer a few moments before serving time.

Invert to unmold. If necessary wrap in warm wet towel.

Homemade Applesauce with Honey

Serves 2

I use buckwheat honey in this recipe because it imparts a unique rich flavor. Experiment with your favorite honey; you may discover an even better combination.

		Calories
2	large McIntosh apples	140
¾	cup water	0
1½	tablespoons raw buckwheat honey	99
⅛	teaspoon cinnamon	0
	a pinch each of nutmeg and cardamom	0
	Total	239
	Total for 1 portion	119½

Core apples, cut them into ½-inch slices and cook in water until they are soft, about 15 minutes.
Remove apple slices and strain into a bowl. Add the remaining ingredients to the cooking water and simmer until the liquid is reduced to 3 tablespoons.
Stir this syrup into the applesauce and top with a sprinkle of cinnamon.
Serve hot or cold.

Sliced Peach with Honey

Generally I consider peeling fruit a sacrilege, but once in a while it may be condoned.

		Calories
1	large ripe peach	35
1	tablespoon honey	66
1	heaping teaspoon yoghurt	3
	a dash of nutmeg	0
	Total	104

Just before serving time, wash the peach, scald it and pull off the skin.
Slice the fruit into a small glass dish. Spoon the honey over it and top with yoghurt and nutmeg.
Serve immediately.

Whole Seckel Pears with Almonds

		Calories
3	Seckel pears	150
1	tablespoon honey	66
¼	cup water	0
⅛	teaspoon cinnamon	0
	a dash of powdered cloves	0
1	tablespoon slivered almonds	53
	Total	269
	Total for 1	90

Peel and core the pears and place them in a rather deep baking dish.

Bring the honey, water, cinnamon and cloves to a boil, then lower heat and cook for 1 minute more.

Pour this syrup over the pears and bake for 50 minutes in an oven preheated to 350°F. Cool to room temperature and refrigerate until time to serve.

Place the pears in a small bowl, pour syrup over them, top with almonds and serve cold.

Apricots in Orange Juice

These are so good I would suggest preparing a double portion.
They should be made two days before you plan to serve them.

		Calories
6	dried apricots	60
½	cup fresh orange juice	56
2	teaspoons honey	44
½	teaspoon rosewater (optional)	0
8	whole blanched almonds	64
	Total	224

Place the apricots, honey and rosewater in a glass bowl.
Pour the orange juice over the fruit.
Refrigerate for 2 days, stirring occasionally.
To serve, stir in the whole almonds.
Serve cold.

Stewed Apricots and Honey

		Calories
6	dried Iranian apricots	58
1	tablespoon honey	66
¼	cup fresh orange juice	28
¼	cup water	0
½	stick cinnamon	0
2	cloves	0
	a pinch of powdered anise	0
	Total	152

Rinse the apricots and place all ingredients in the top of a glass double boiler.
Simmer until the fruit is fairly soft and the syrup is thick.
Serve warm or cold.
Save the cinnamon stick to nibble on when you're tempted to cheat on your diet and want to have an illegal sweet.

Spanish Orange Slices

		Calories
		Calories
1	large orange	60
1	teaspoon raw buckwheat honey	22
¼	cup fresh orange juice	28
⅛	teaspoon cinnamon	0
	Total	110

Peel the orange carefully, removing all of the white pith. Cut into ½-inch slices.
Place the orange slices in a small glass bowl. Mix the honey with the orange juice and pour this over the sliced fruit.
Sprinkle with cinnamon and refrigerate for 1 hour.
Serve cold.

Strawberries in Honeydew Melon

Other fruits may be substituted for the strawberries, but check the calorie chart to make sure the count is approximately the same.

		Calories
½	honeydew melon	100
¾	cup strawberries	42
1	teaspoon honey	22
	Total	164

Remove the seeds from the half melon.
Wash and hull the strawberries and place them in the hollowed-out center of the melon.
Dribble honey over the berries.
Serve cold.

Healthy Strawberries Romanov

		Calories
1	cup ripe strawberries	55
1	small orange	60
1	tablespoon yoghurt	8
½	teaspoon organic raw sugar	8½
	Total	131½

Wash and hull strawberries. Place them in a glass dish and squeeze orange juice over them.
Refrigerate for at least ½ hour, turning once.
To serve, top with yoghurt and sprinkle with sugar.
Serve at once.

Baked Apple with Dates and Nuts

		Calories
1	large McIntosh apple	70
3	dates	15
6	pecan halves	22
1	teaspoon organic raw sugar	17
	a sprinkle of ground cloves	0
¼	teaspoon butter	8
	Total	132

Remove the seeds and core from the apple without cutting through the blossom end. Scoop some of the pulp from the apple and chop it along with the dates and nuts. Sprinkle this filling with sugar and cloves and mix well.
Use this to fill the hollow of the apple. Top with butter.
Pour warm water into an ovenproof dish until it reaches the level of ½ inch.
Place the apple in the water and bake for 40 minutes in an oven preheated to 400°F. The apple should be soft but not mushy.
Serve hot or cold.

Baked Apple with Raisins and Prunes

		Calories
1	large McIntosh apple	70
1	heaping tablespoon golden raisins	35
3	prunes, pitted	51
1	teaspoon organic raw sugar	17
	a pinch each cinnamon and nutmeg	0
	Total	173

Remove the seeds and core from the apple without cutting through the blossom end.

Scoop some of the pulp from the apple and chop it along with the raisins and the pitted prunes.

Sprinkle this filling with the sugar, cinnamon and nutmeg, and mix well.

Fill the hollow of the apple and top with butter.

Pour warm water into an ovenproof dish until it reaches the level of ½ inch.

Place the apple in the water and bake for 40 minutes in an oven preheated to 400°F. The apple should be soft but not mushy.

Serve hot or cold.

Baked Bananas

Natural fruit flavors from the West Indies enhance this delicious dessert.

		Calories
2	red bananas or barely ripe yellow ones	170
⅓	cup orange juice	37
1	tablespoon honey	66
	a small pinch of nutmeg	0
1	teaspoon grated coconut	8
	Total	281

Peel bananas and cut them in half lengthwise. Dip them in orange juice and place them, cut-side down, in a glass baking dish. Pour orange juice and honey into the bottom of the dish but not over the bananas. Sprinkle with nutmeg.
Bake in an oven preheated to 400°F. for 10 minutes. Remove from oven and immediately use tongs to turn fruit in the syrup in the bottom of the dish. Lift the baked bananas onto a *lightly* oiled plate. Sprinkle with coconut.
Serve warm or cold.

Baked Divinity Squares

		Calories
¼	cup organic raw sugar	204
1	tablespoon honey	66
¼	cup boiling water	0
1	tablespoon butter	100
½	vanilla bean	0
1	egg	75
5	dried apricots	50
8	raw cashew nuts	80
2	tablespoons sesame seeds	80
	Total	655
	Total for 1	81

Place the sugar, honey, water, butter and vanilla bean in an enamel pan and stir until the sugar is dissolved.

Cook over medium heat until the syrup reaches the soft-ball stage (240°F. on a candy thermometer).

Separate the egg white from the yolk. Beat the white until it stands in peaks.

Beat the syrup into the egg white. Add the yolk and beat once more.

Chop the apricots and the nuts and add them, with the sesame seeds, to the egg mixture. Spoon into a greased loaf pan and bake for 35–40 minutes in an oven preheated to 350°F.

Remove from the oven and cool for 15 minutes. Cut into 8 pieces and cool to room temperature. Remove the pieces from the pan and wrap them in waxed paper.

Cottage Cheese Pancakes

Makes 6 cakes

Have 3 of these delicious Russian delicacies for dinner to-night and 3 tomorrow night . . . they reheat beautifully—or better still, share them with a friend.

		Calories
½	cup cottage cheese	98
1	teaspoon safflower oil	42
2	tablespoons whole wheat flour	50
1	tablespoon organic raw sugar	51
1	egg	75
1	teaspoon wheat germ	5
½	teaspoon nutritional yeast	3
4	pecan halves, finely chopped	64
½	teaspoon sesame seeds	5
⅛	teaspoon each cinnamon and salt	0
3	teaspoons yoghurt	
3	teaspoons honey	

Total	393
Total for 1	65
Total for 3 with yoghurt and honey	207

Beat together all ingredients except yoghurt and honey.
Oil a baking sheet and spread the batter to form 6 pancakes or patties.
Sprinkle with cinnamon. Bake for 25 minutes in an oven pre-heated to 350°F.
Spread each pancake with ½ teaspoon of yoghurt and ½ tea-spoon of honey.
Serve warm.

Vigor Fruit and Nut Loaf

Makes 6 slices

		Calories
1	cup Vigor Cereal (see recipe, page 42)	400
1	egg yolk	60
1	tablespoon honey	66
2	tablespoons Tiger Milk Powder (carob flavor)	124
1	tablespoon milk	10
¼	cup pecan halves	149
½	cup raisins	140
½	cup chopped pitted prunes	280
¼	teaspoon cinnamon	0
⅛	teaspoon nutmeg	0
	a generous sprinkle of powdered cloves	0
	Total	1229
	Total for 1 slice	205

Beat all ingredients together in a large bowl.
Spoon batter into a buttered loaf pan.
Bake for 45 to 55 minutes in an oven preheated to 350°F.

Cashew Custard Pudding

Serves 2

Warm, mellow and rich is this nutritious custard.

		Calories
8	raw cashew nuts	80
1	1-inch cube goat's cheese	70
2	tablespoons dried brown-bread crumbs	26
¾	cup milk	120
1	teaspoon butter	33
1	egg	75
1½	tablespoons organic raw sugar	75
	a pinch of sea salt	0
½	teaspoon grated orange zest (orange outer skin with none of the white pulp)	0
⅛	teaspoon cinnamon	0
1	teaspoon honey	22
	Total	501
	Total for 1	250

Grate nuts and cheese together. Place half the nuts and cheese in the bottom of a small, ovenproof bowl. Sprinkle half the bread crumbs over them and repeat, using the remainder of the nuts and cheese and bread crumbs.

Scald the milk with the butter. Beat together the egg, sugar, salt and orange zest. Slowly stir in the hot milk and butter. Spoon this over the cheese, nuts and bread crumbs and sprinkle with cinnamon.

Place the bowl in a cake pan with 1 inch of hot water in it. Bake for 40 minutes in an oven preheated to 350°F., or until the custard is set.

Serve warm with ½ teaspoon of honey on each portion.

Vigor Chewies

Makes 8 cookies

		Calories
1	cup Vigor Cereal (see recipe, page 42)	400
1	egg white	15
1	tablespoon shredded coconut	22
1	tablespoon Tiger's Milk powder (carob flavor)	62
½	teaspoon cinnamon	0
	Total	499
	Total for 1	62

Measure cereal into bowl.
Beat egg white until it is stiff but not dry.
Mix cereal, coconut, Tiger's Milk and cinnamon.
Fold in egg white.
Drop spoonful by spoonful on a greased cookie sheet.
Bake for 10 minutes in an oven preheated to 350°F.
Remove cookies from cookie sheet with a spatula and place on a plate to cool.

Low Carbohydrate Desserts

Unfortunately, sweet desserts are practically taboo in a low carbohydrate diet.

Here are a few, just in case you feel you simply can't abstain a moment longer. It would be wise, however, to begin to develop the strength of will to put sweets out of your daily food regimen completely. Train your taste buds to appreciate the subtle sweetness in a single dried apricot or a slice of apple. Once you renounce white sugars and starches, you will find yourself released from degrading servitude to your sweet tooth.

Strawberries with Sugar

		Carbohydrates
1	cup fresh medium-sized strawberries (about 20)	13
1	beaten egg white	tr
2½	tablespoons organic raw sugar	7½
	Total	20½
	Total for 1	1

Rinse and dry berries, retaining stems.
Beat the egg white until frothy.
Spread the sugar on a saucer. Dip the berries in egg white and then in sugar.
Dry for 20 minutes.
Chill briefly.
Serve cold.

Dried Apricots with Pecans

		Carbohydrates
1	egg white	tr
8	dried apricots	20
2	tablespoons finely chopped pecans	2
	Total	22
	Total for 1	3

Beat the egg white until it is frothy.
Dip the apricots in egg white and then in nuts.
Dry on paper towels for 30 minutes.
Refrigerate.

Dessert Tempura

Better serve this as a company dessert or you may find you're tempted to overindulge.

Carbohydrates

BATTER

2	tablespoons whole wheat flour	6
2	tablespoons rice polish	0
¼	cup ice-cold water	0
½	beaten egg	tr
	oil for deep frying	0
	organic raw sugar	0
	Total	6
	Batter for 1 tidbit	½

TIDBITS *

1	1-inch piece fresh pineapple	tr
1	slice apple	tr
½	dried apricot	tr
1	strawberry	tr
1	2-inch by ¼-inch slice pumpkin	tr

Beat together the flour, rice polish, water and egg.
Shake tidbits in a bag with 2 tablespoons of flour to make sure the batter will cover completely.
Dip the fruit tidbits in the cold batter and drop into 3 inches of hot oil (350°F.). Fry until golden.
Serve immediately, sprinkled with a few grains of sugar.

* Add the carbohydrate count of each "tidbit" plus the "batter for 1 tidbit" count.

snacks

Low Calorie Snacks

Fruit Snacks

Makes 7

		Calories
10	prunes	70
¼	cup shelled pecan halves	149
	the zest or thin outer skin of an orange, no white included	0
	a generous pinch each ground anise and cloves	0
2	tablespoons organic raw sugar	102
	Total	321
	Total for 1	46

Chop together finely the prunes, pecans and orange zest.
Add the spices and mix well. Shape into 7 "fingers," each approximately 2½ inches by ½ inch. Roll each fruit finger in sugar.
Roll each in a small piece of plastic wrap.

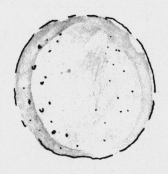

Stuffed Dates

Less is more if it's rich and sweet. Eat one of these with a cup of herb tea and be satisfied.

		Calories
3	unsulfured dates	15
1½	teaspoons cream cheese	27
3	walnut quarters	33
3	pinches organic raw sugar	3
	Total	78
	Total for 1	26

Slit the dates and stuff each with ½ teaspoon of cream cheese. Top with a walnut quarter and a pinch of sugar.

Nutty Apple Slices

Makes approximately 15 slices

		Calories
1	medium-sized apple	70
1	tablespoon lemon juice	5
½	tablespoon cream cheese	26
1	tablespoon cottage cheese	12
1	tablespoon finely chopped pecans	50
¼	teaspoon cinnamon	0
	Total	163
	Total for 1 slice	11

Core apple and cut in slices, but do not peel.
Toss the apple slices in lemon juice.
Mix the cream cheese, cottage cheese and nuts.
Spread the slices with the cheese mixture.
Sprinkle with cinnamon, if desired.
Refrigerate.
Serve cold.

Broiled Grapefruit

		Calories
½	grapefruit	55
1	teaspoon honey	22
¼	teaspoon wheat germ	1
	a pinch each of nutmeg and cinnamon	0
	Total	78

Remove seeds and center core and loosen the sections of one grapefruit half. Top with honey, wheat germ and spices.
Broil several inches from the flame for 10 minutes.
Serve hot.

Yoghurt with Apple
and Winter Wheat Sprouts

The winter wheat sprouts give this dessert (or afternoon snack) its unusual and delicious flavor.

		Calories
1	6-ounce glass plain yoghurt	90
1	tablespoon primeval flowers honey (or any other)	66
½	apple	35
1	tablespoon winter wheat sprouts	1
	Total	192

Place cold yoghurt in an 8-ounce glass and spoon in the honey.
Peel the apple, grate it, and add it to the yoghurt. Stir gently.
Top with sprouts and serve cold.

Walnut Snacks

Makes 16

Don't reach for a cookie; reach for one of these nutrition-laden walnut treats. Tiger's Milk powder is substituted for flour to produce a sweet with nearly as much pick-me-up as a vitamin pill.

		Calories
2	egg whites	30
9	dates	45
½	cup shelled walnut halves	325
5	heaping tablespoons Tiger's Milk powder	124
1	tablespoon wheat germ	15
½	cup unsulfured golden raisins	280
½	cup unsulfured dark raisins	280
1	tablespoon honey	66
½	teaspoon powdered cinnamon	0
¼	teaspoon ground nutmeg	0
	Total	1165
	Total for 1	73

Beat egg whites until they hold a soft point when the beater is raised.

Chop dates coarsely. Stir all ingredients together. Use your fingers to form into 16 balls. Place on a greased cookie sheet and bake for 12 minutes at 350°F.

Remove from oven and allow to cool before wrapping each in plastic wrap fastened with a piece of pipe cleaner.

Sesame Squares

Makes 8 squares

		Calories
¼	cup sesame seeds	160
½	teaspoon orange zest (the thin outer skin, no white included)	0
10	pecan halves, chopped	100
1	egg	75
¼	cup organic raw sugar	204
3	tablespoons whole wheat flour	75
⅛	teaspoon sea salt	0
8	pecan halves	80
	Total	694
	Total for 1	87

Place sesame seeds, orange zest and chopped pecans on a chopping board.

Add the egg, sugar, flour and sea salt and mix thoroughly with your fingers. Place this batter in the bottom of an oiled loaf pan, and arrange the pecan halves neatly in 2 evenly spaced rows.

Bake for 25 minutes in an oven preheated to 350°F. Remove from the oven and cool for 5 minutes.

Cut into squares with a pecan half in the center of each. Loosen the edges, carefully lift the squares and arrange them on a plate until they are cool.

Honey–Coconut Balls

Makes 10 1-inch balls

When you feel an irresistible urge for something extra sweet—
try these. But remember, these calories *do* count.

		Calories
2	tablespoons honey	132
2	teaspoons organic raw sugar	34
3	tablespoons water	0
2	tablespoons shredded coconut	44
2	tablespoons raisins	70
4	dried apricot halves, coarsely chopped	39
2	tablespoons sunflower seeds	42
	Total	361
	Total for 1	36

Mix honey, sugar and water in a small enamel pan.
Boil over medium heat until the syrup forms a soft ball when
a small amount is dropped into a glass of cold water.
Quickly stir in coconut, raisins, apricots and sunflower seeds.
Grease a plate and your hands, and form the candy into 1-inch
balls.
Wrap each in plastic wrap, twist at the top to secure, and nibble
when sugar mania strikes.

Cottage Cheese Nibbles

Makes 10

Here's a different and most delicious way to enjoy cottage cheese.

		Calories
3	dates	15
1	watermelon pickle, 1-inch square	2
10	cashews	100
3	tablespoons cottage cheese	48
1½	teaspoons organic raw sugar	25
¼	teaspoon cinnamon	0
	Total	190
	Total for 1	19

Finely chop dates, pickle and nuts.
Mix with cottage cheese. Shape into 10 small balls.
Roll in sugar and cinnamon.
Refrigerate.

Dill-Stuffed Eggs

		Calories
1	hard-cooked egg	75
1	teaspoon finely chopped onion	1
1	teaspoon fresh dill weed, finely chopped	0
½	teaspoon yoghurt mayonnaise (see page 33)	3
⅛	teaspoon sea salt	0
1	teaspoon toasted pumpkin seed kernels	10
	Total	89
	Total for 1 half	45

Split hard-cooked egg lengthwise and remove yolk.
Force the yolk through a fine sieve and mix with onion, dill, yoghurt mayonnaise and sea salt.
Fill the whites with this mixture and decorate with pumpkin seed kernels standing up like porcupine quills.
Chill.
Serve cold.

Deviled Dandelion Eggs

		Calories
3	hard-cooked eggs	225
2	tablespoons finely chopped young dandelion leaves	1
1	tablespoon yoghurt mayonnaise (see page 33)	19
⅛	teaspoon each dry mustard and nutmeg	0
	Total	245
	Total for 1 half egg	41

Cut the eggs in half lengthwise.
Force the yolks through a fine sieve.
Mix the sieved egg yolks, dandelion leaves, yoghurt mayonnaise and spices.
Fill the egg whites, using a pastry tube if available.
Chill.
Serve cold.

Avocado Balls

Makes approximately 10

Double this recipe for a tasty company snack.

		Calories
½	ripe avocado	185
1	tablespoon safflower oil	125
2	tablespoons lemon juice	8
½	clove garlic, crushed	0
¼	teaspoon chili powder	0
	Total with excess marinade discarded	318
	Total for 1	31

Remove the avocado pulp with a melon-ball cutter.
Mix the oil, lemon juice, garlic and chili powder.
Place the avocado balls in a glass bowl and pour the lemon juice marinade over them. Stir.
Chill for several hours, stirring occasionally.
Drain, insert a wooden pick in each, and serve cold.

Low Carbohydrate Snacks

Stuffed Mushrooms
with Pumpkin Seed Kernels

These tiny, raw mushrooms have a creamy cheese filling and the pumpkin seed kernels stand up like porcupine quills.

		Carbohydrates
10	very small, fresh mushrooms	2
2	tablespoons cream cheese	tr
2	tablespoons grated goat's cheese	tr
⅛	teaspoon curry powder	0
1	tablespoon pumpkin seed kernels	1½
	Total	3½
	Total for 1	tr or 0

Rinse the mushrooms. Remove and finely mince the stems.
Drain the mushroom caps on paper towels.
Mix the cream cheese, goat's cheese, curry powder and minced mushroom stems.
Fill the mushroom caps with this mixture and decorate with pumpkin seed kernels standing upright.
Serve cold.

Cold Shrimp Balls

		Carbohydrates
¼	pound boiled shrimp, shelled and deveined	0
2	hard-cooked eggs, shelled	tr
¼	teaspoon sea salt	0
⅛	teaspoon pepper	0
¼	teaspoon dill weed	0
1½	tablespoons sour cream	1
1	tablespoon wheat germ	2
	Total	3
	Total for 1	tr

Finely chop the shrimp and the hard-cooked eggs.
Mix the shrimp, eggs, spices and sour cream.
Form into small balls and roll in wheat germ.
Refrigerate.
Serve cold.

Alfalfa Sprout Nibbles

		Carbohydrates
¼	cup alfalfa sprouts	1
¼	cup cream cheese	2
¼	cup chopped unblanched almonds	6
¼	teaspoon sea salt	0
	a generous pinch of curry powder	0
	Total	9

Coarsely chop the alfalfa sprouts.
Mix the sprouts, cream cheese, 2 tablespoons of the chopped nuts, the salt and curry powder.
Shape into balls and roll in the remaining chopped nuts.
Chill.
Serve cold.

Tongue Pinwheels

Makes approximately 20

		Carbohydrates
10	thin slices tongue	0
¼	pound cream cheese	4
⅛	teaspoon curry powder	0
1	tablespoon chopped raw cashews	1
	Total	5
	Total for 1	tr

Trim tongue slices and spread each with cream cheese.
Roll up tightly, cut in half and fasten with toothpicks.
Squeeze each gently in the middle to force out a little of the cream cheese.
Dip the ends in chopped nuts and refrigerate.
Serve cold.

Cold Turkey Rolls

		Carbohydrates
1	tablespoon butter	tr
1	tablespoon cream cheese	tr
1	teaspoon wheat germ	½
1	tablespoon chopped raw cashews	20
4	very thin roast turkey slices	0
8	sprigs watercress	0
	Total	20½
	Total for 1	5

Cream together the butter, cream cheese and wheat germ.
Stir in the nuts and spread the mixture on the turkey slices.
Arrange the sprigs of watercress stem to stem, so that the leaves
stick out at each end when the turkey slices are rolled.
Fasten with a toothpick and chill.
Serve cold.

Grandma's Pickled Eggs

Ideal for a snack or for a picnic lunch are these old-fashioned red pickled eggs.

		Carbohydrates
3	medium-sized beets	12
5	hard-cooked eggs	tr
1	cup cider vinegar	32
2	tablespoons organic raw sugar	6
1	clove garlic, crushed	0
1	teaspoon pickling spices	0
½	teaspoon sea salt	0
	Total	50
	Total with marinade discarded	15
	Total for 1 egg*	1
	Total for ¼ beet	1

Cook the beets in an enamel pot until tender.
Peel the beets and cut them in quarters.
Shell the hard-cooked eggs. Mix the beet quarters, vinegar, sugar, garlic, pickling spices and sea salt, and allow to stand for 45 minutes.
Place the shelled eggs in a quart jar. Add the beets with their marinade and refrigerate for a day or two—or even a week.

* Each egg absorbs a small amount of sugar from the marinade.

Pickled Mushrooms

		Carbohydrates
20	small, fresh mushrooms	10
2	tablespoons lemon juice	2
2	tablespoons safflower oil	0
1	scallion with 3 inches green top, chopped	1
½	teaspoon sea salt	0
⅛	teaspoon pepper	0
	Total	13
	Total with marinade discarded	11
	Total for 1	½

Rinse mushrooms.
Mix remaining ingredients.
Add mushrooms and refrigerate for at least 2 days, stirring occasionally.
Serve cold.

Peanut Butter and Sunflower Seed Celery

		Carbohydrates
2	8-inch stalks celery without leaves	10
2	tablespoons organic peanut butter	6
1	teaspoon wheat germ	½
⅛	teaspoon sea salt	0
1	tablespoon sunflower seeds	1
	Total	17½
	Total for ½ piece	5

Rinse and dry celery.

Mix the peanut butter, wheat germ and sea salt, and use this to stuff the celery.

Cut each piece of stuffed celery in half and sprinkle with sunflower seeds.

Chill and serve cold.

Sweet Soy Nuts

		Carbohydrates
1	cup pecan halves	16
1	tablespoon butter	tr
1	tablespoon soy sauce	1
2	teaspoons organic raw sugar	2
	Total	19
	Total for 10 nuts	2½

Melt the butter in a skillet.
Add the pecan halves and stir over medium heat for 1 minute.
Sprinkle with soy sauce and sugar, and continue to stir until the soy sauce disappears and the nuts are coated.
Cool, dry on paper towels and store in a glass jar.

Additional Low Carbohydrate Snacks

		Carbohydrates
1	wedge cheese, 2 inches by ½ inch	tr
1	hard-cooked egg	tr
1	thin, rolled slice of meat	0
1	shrimp	0
1	ounce crabmeat	tr
	bits of fish with lemon juice	0
1	radish rose	tr
1	slice zucchini or summer squash dipped in sour cream	tr

drinks

Wintergreen or Teaberry Tea

When I was a child, I looked upon the teaberry plant as my own secret treasure. Hidden away in the still forests, these glossy green leaves with the cheery, cherry-red berries provided a refreshing nibble on many a brisk hike. Just when it seemed the next hill was surely too high to scramble up, I would remember the treat that nature so thoughtfully provided. Today, any hint of wintergreen brings to mind those tender times when our now-threatened forests seemed vast and invincible.

		Calories	Carbohydrates
10	teaberry leaves	0	0
1½	cups boiling water	0	0
	Total	0	0

Crush or crumble the leaves and place them in a small glass or enamel pot.
Pour boiling water over the leaves and allow to steep for 3 minutes.
Strain into a teacup.
Sweeten with honey or organic raw sugar.

Spicy Mint Tea

		Calories	Carbohydrates
1½	cups boiling water	0	0
½	stick cinnamon	0	0
2	whole cloves	0	0
2	whole allspice	0	0
1	teaspoon mint leaves	0	0
	Total	0	0

Bring water, cinnamon, cloves and allspice to a boil in a glass or enamel pan.
Boil for 1 minute. Stir in mint leaves.
Remove from heat and steep for 3 minutes.
Strain into cup.
Sweeten with honey, if desired.

Sassafras Tea

I look upon northeastern Pennsylvania as a land of plenty. Most of my childhood was spent there, and I cherish memories of fruit-laden orchards and field after golden field of heavy, rippling grain. One of the pleasant bounties nature provided was a sassafras tree which grew just around the bend from my house, near the edge of the forest. The rust-colored sassafras roots provided us with many a pot of fragrant tea.

Ahh, sassafras—warming in the winter, cooling when iced in the summer, and marvelous as a spring tonic.

		Calories	Carbohydrates
2	pieces sassafras root (or bark)	0	0
2	cups boiling water	0	0
	Total	0	0

Scrub roots and cut into short pieces.
Place the roots and water in a glass or enamel pot.
Boil for 15 minutes or until the tea is red and strong.
Serve hot, sweetened with honey or organic raw sugar, or chill and serve with ice.

Flower Tea

It's worth growing and drying your own flowers if it means a winter's worth of this lovely tea.

	Calories	Carbohydrates
Equal portions of		
flowers of elder	0	0
flowers of blue malva	0	0
small rose petals	0	0
yarrow	0	0
lavender	0	0
life everlasting	0	0
camomile	0	0
sassafras root	0	0
Total	0	0

Dry flowers in a dark, dry, warm, clean place. Grind sassafras root. Mix carefully. Store in an airtight glass jar so the tea will retain its subtle flavor and you may admire its beauty.

Orange–Prune Pickup

High in quick energy and nutrition, this shake could substitute for breakfast, lunch or dessert.

		Calories
⅓	cup orange juice	37
⅓	cup unsweetened prune juice	66
2	teaspoons honey	44
1	teaspoon wheat germ	5
2	ice cubes	0
	Total	152

Place all ingredients in the container of your blender.
Blend until ice is finely cracked.
Serve immediately.

Cran–Orange Pickup

This refreshing drink could substitute for lunch on any really hectic day.

		Calories
⅔	cup orange juice	74
¼	cup fresh cranberries	50
1	tablespoon honey	66
1	tablespoon yoghurt	8
2	ice cubes	0
	Total	198

Place all ingredients in the container of your blender. Blend until smooth and frothy.
Serve immediately.

Tomato–Yoghurt Pickup

This drink is a meal in itself.

		Calories
1	small, ripe tomato	25
¼	small onion	10
½	cup basic vegetable stock (see page 38)	40
⅓	cup yoghurt	40
1	teaspoon wheat germ	5
1	egg yolk	60
	sea salt to taste	0
	a pinch of dill weed	0
2	ice cubes	0
	Total	180

Chop tomato and onion and place in blender container with remaining ingredients.
Blend until fairly smooth.
Drink or eat with a spoon.

Non-Alcoholic Eggnog

If your carbohydrate count is particularly low today, you might indulge in this rich, creamy eggnog.

		Carbohydrates
½	cup milk	6
½	cup cream	3
1	egg yolk	tr
2	teaspoons buckwheat honey	6
⅛	teaspoon nutmeg	0
	Total	15

Place all ingredients in the container of your blender.
Blend on low speed for 20 seconds.
Serve cold with a little whipped cream on top if desired.

Strawberry Mint Cooler

		Carbohydrates
1	teaspoon fresh mint leaves	0
½	cup strawberries	1½
¼	cup cream	2
¼	cup milk	3
2	ice cubes	0
	Total	6½

Rinse and hull strawberries.
Place in blender.
Blend until smooth.
Serve immediately topped with a mint sprig.

appendix

Where to Obtain
Natural and Organic Foods
by Mail

Write for the *Organic Directory*, Rodale Press, Emmaus, Pa., for additional sources.

General Supplies

Arkansas
Shiloh Farms, Sulphur Springs, Ark. 72768

California
Erewhon Trading Corp., 8003 Beverly Blvd., Los Angeles, Calif. 90048
Jaffe Brothers, P.O. Box 636, Valley Center, Calif. 92082

Colorado
General Nutrition Corp., New Englewood Mall, Denver, Colo. 80201

New York
Deer Valley Farm, Guilford, N.Y. 13780
White Plains Nutrition Center, 420 Mamaroneck Ave., White Plains, N.Y. 10605

Pennsylvania
Walnut Acres, Penns Creek, Pa. 17862
Natural Sales Co., P.O. Box 25, Pittsburgh, Pa. 15230

Specialties

Apples
Golden Acres Orchard, Box 70, Rte. 2, Front Royal, Va. 22630

Apples, Pears, Grapes, Rose Hips, Nuts
Organic Foods Research Farms, Box 304, Rte. 3, Dayton, Ohio 37321

Breads, Whole Grain
Mease's Natural Foods, Inc., Shoeneck, Pa. 17574

Citrus Fruits
Cartwright Groves, Box 331, Carrizo Springs, Tex. 78834

Citrus Fruits, Sweet Potatoes
Lee's Fruit Co., Box 450, Leesburg, Fla. 32748

Citrus Fruits, Dates, Date Products, Pecans
Lee Anderson's Covalda Date Co., P.O. Box 908, Coachella, Calif.
92236

Citrus Fruits, Pineapples
Nightingale Organic Grove and Nursery, Box 847, Rte. 1, Punta Gorda,
Fla. 33950

Fruits
Jefferson Organic Orchards, Box 224, Rte. 1, Mission, Tex. 78572

Goat Cheese
Diamond Dairy Goat Farm, P.O. Box 133, North Prairie, Wis. 53153

Grains
Arrowhead Mills, Box 866, Hereford, Tex. 79045

Herbs and Herb Teas
Pine Hills Herb Farm, P.O. Box 307, Roswell, Ga. 30075
Desert Herb Tea Co., 736 Darling St., Ogden, Utah 84403
Indiana Botanic Gardens, Hammond, Ind. 46325

Honey
Ault Bee Farm, Box 23, Rte. 3, Weslaco, Tex. 78596
Lang Apiaries, Gasport, N.Y. 14067
Lyman Apiaries, Greenwich, N.Y. 12834
Thousand Island Apiaries, Clayton, N.Y. 13624
Yack Brothers Honey Co., Roosevelt, Utah 84066

Jerusalem Artichokes
Vita-Green Farms, P.O. Box 878, Vista, Calif. 92083

Kefir Grains
R.A.J. Biological Laboratory, 35 Park Ave., Blue Point, N.Y. 11715

Meats
Wolf's Neck Farms, Freeport, Me. 04082

Nuts
Hazel Hills Nursery, Rte. 1, River Falls, Wis. 54022
James Pecan Farm, Highway 24, Brunswick, Mo. 65236

glossary

Unusual Foods

Adzuki beans
Beautiful, small, shiny red beans from northern Japan.

Alfalfa leaves
Leaves rich in calcium, iron, phosphorus, sodium, sulfur and vitamins A, B, C, D, E and K. Recommended as a healthful herb tea when dried.

Alfalfa sprouts
Delicious, crisp, healthful sprouts of the alfalfa seed.

Arame
A variety of seawood used as a vegetable.

Black beans
A bean used mostly in sauces. It has a rich, dark color and a sweet flavor.

Bonito flakes
Flesh of the bonito fish which has been dried and shaved. Used as a flavoring in Japanese foods.

Brown rice
Natural rice. The best is short-grained and milled carefully so that the outer coat is not broken. Contains the nutritive outer coating lacking in white rice.

Bulghour
A processed wheat from the Near East.

Burdock
A wild root vegetable.

Cellophane Noodles
Thin, transparent Chinese noodles made from the mung bean.

Couscous
A processed wheat similar to BULGHOUR. Served mostly in Morocco.

Daikon
White, Japanese radish. Dried.

Dandelion greens
Young, green leaves from this plant have a rather bitter but pleasant flavor. They are very rich in vitamin A and in the B vitamins.

Dulse
One of the salty seaweeds. Good in soups.

Garbanzo beans
Chickpeas. A fat bean popular in the Near East.

Hiziki
Small, black seaweed, spindle-shaped. Used as a vegetable.

Kasha
Cracked buckwheat, barley or millet.

Kombu
A thick green seaweed that comes packaged in sheets. Usually cut in strips, tied in knots and cooked in soups.

Miso
A soybean paste or purée made from fermented soybeans. This salty paste takes three years to make.

Mung sprouts
Sprouts from the mung bean. Traditionally used in Chinese cooking.

Mustard sprouts
Sprouts from the mustard seed. Very fine and hot in flavor.

Nasturtium flowers
Flowers from the nasturtium plant. These are also quite hot to the taste and are good in salads.

Nasturtium leaves
Leaves from the nasturtium plant. These have a hot flavor and are good in salads.

Navy beans
A small white bean used in making soups.

Nori
A kind of seaweed.

Nutritional yeast
A nonrising yeast rich in minerals. Used to bolster the nutritional content of foods.

Pink beans
An inexpensive and tasty bean used in making baked beans.

Pinto beans
An attractive bean used in Mexican cooking. It is inexpensive and high in calcium and phosphorus.

Sea salt
Salt made by the evaporation of sea water. It contains no additives.

Seaweed
This vegetable from the sea comes in many varieties. Hiziki, Dulse, Kombu, Nori, and Wakame are a few. Generally salty in taste, most seaweed should be soaked in several waters, then cut and used in cooking. If a small bit is to be used in a soup or stew there is no need to soak.

Seitan
A dried product made from soybeans. It resembles beef jerky and is used to produce a beef-like taste.

Semolina
The flour made from the hardest part of the wheat.

Soba
Buckwheat noodles used in Japanese cooking.

Soybeans
A versatile and nutritious bean used to make soy milk, soy cheese, soy lecithin, etc. An excellent substitute for meat because of its protein, vitamin and mineral content, combined with its inexpensive price.

Soy sauce
A by-product of miso, soy sauce is a concentrated, salty liquid. Commercial brands are thought to be damaging to the health. Use the brands you find in your health foods store.

Tahini
Sesame butter. Made of hulled sesame seeds ground to a paste.

Tamari
See SOY SAUCE.

Tempura
Deep fried, batter-dipped fish and vegetables native to Japan but now very popular in the U.S.A.

Tofu
Soybean curd made from the liquid of crushed soybeans.

Udon
A kind of vermicelli made of cornmeal. Used in Japanese cooking.

Umeboshi plums
Plums preserved in salt for three years.

Wakame
A kind of seaweed

Yeast
(Nutritional) Primary dried food yeast. The flavor of various brands varies considerably. A good brand is Redstar Milwaukee.

Herbs and Spices

Anise
A licorice-flavored seed used in cooking or as a tea for reducing nausea.

Basil
A sweet leaf with a slight anise flavor.

Bay leaf
A strong-tasting dried leaf used to flavor sauces and stews.

Cardamom
A spice that also serves as a breath sweetener.

Comfrey
Used for ulcers and coughs. Rich in calcium and potassium.

Coriander
Ground seeds flavor bread, sausages, etc. One ingredient of curry powder.

Cumin
A hot-tasting ground seed. One ingredient of curry powder.

Dandelion
A wild plant used in salads. High in vitamins A, B_1, C and E, calcium, potasium and magnesium.

Dill
A weed that often grows wild. Used to flavor fish dishes.

Fennel
A spice with a licorice flavor. The leaves are good in salads.

Garlic
A strong-smelling and tasting bulb of the lily family.

Ginger root
A spicy rhizomatous tropical plant used in oriental cooking.

Horseradish
A root strong in flavor. Grated, it is used to enliven beef and fish dishes.

Lavender
A sweet-smelling flower used in sachets.

Marjoram
A spice useful in flavoring sauces.

Nutmeg
When these kernels are ground, they are delicious in desserts as well as meat and fish dishes. Also considered as a stimulant.

Oregano
Produces a zesty flavor. Used frequently in Italian cooking.

Paprika
A spice that comes from the ripe fruit of a mild red pepper.

Parsley
A small, green plant with ruffled leaves. Extremely versatile.

Peppermint
Refreshing either dried or fresh in salads and sauces.

Rosemary
A sweet herb used to flavor meat stews and sauces.

Saffron
An extremely expensive spice used in dishes native to India. It is distinctive in flavor and bright yellow in color.

Sage
A spice useful in flavoring meat and vegetable sauces and stews.

Thyme
A delicately flavored spice that enhances almost any meat, fish, egg or cheese recipe. Also considered as a stimulant.

Dried Fruits, Nuts and Seeds

Apples	Figs	Prunes
Apricots	Peaches	Raisins
Dates	Pears	
Almonds	Filberts	Pecans
Brazil nuts	Hickory nuts	Pignolias
Cashews	Peanuts	Walnuts
Caraway	Pumpkin	Sunflower
Poppy	Sesame	

Cereals

Barley	Couscous	Rye, flaked
Brown rice	Farina	Semolina
Buckwheat	Millet	Soy grits
Bulghour	Oats	Wheat, flaked
Cornmeal	Rice, flaked	Wheat germ

Flours

Barley	Millet	Soy
Buckwheat	Rice	Wheat, unbleached
Corn	Rye	Wheat, whole
Oat		

Greens

Arugula
Broccoli leaves
Beet tops
Cabbage, green and red
Carrot tops
Chicory
Chinese cabbage
Comfrey
Dandelion
Endive
Escarole
Fennel
Green onions
Kohlrabi leaves

Lettuce
Mustard greens
Nasturtium leaves and flowers
Pepper grass
Purslane
Romaine
Scallions
Shallots
Spinach
Swiss chard
Turnip tops
Watercress
Yarrow, young

Herb Teas

Alfalfa leaf
Anise seed
Bee balm
Birch bark
Blackberry leaf
Blueberry leaf
Camomile
Caraway seed
Celery leaf
Celery seed
Clover blossom
Comfrey leaf
Coriander seed
Costmary leaf
Dill

Elderberry blossom
Fennel seed
Fenugreek seed
Hyssop leaf
Licorice root
Linden blossom
Mint leaf
Nettle
Parsley
Rose hip
Rue leaves
Sage
Sassafras root
Shave gress
Wintergreen

calorie and carbohydrate chart

A

	Calories	Carbohydrates
Adzuki beans, uncooked, ½ cup	297	54
Alfalfa sprouts:		
¼ cup	4	¾
1 tablespoon	1	0
Almonds:		
chopped, 10 whole, ½ ounce, 2		
tablespoons	106	3
chopped, 40 whole, 2 ounces	424	14
shelled, 1 cup	845	27½
slivered, 1 tablespoon	53	2
whole, 1	8	tr
American cheese:		
1-inch cube	70	tr
grated, 1 tablespoon	30	tr
Apple juice, apple cider, bottled or canned,		
1 cup	120	30
Apples, 1 medium, 2½-inch diameter	70	18
Applesauce:		
sweetened, 1 cup	230	60
unsweetened, 1 cup	100	26
Apricot nectar, canned, 1 cup	140	36
Apricots:		
3 medium	55	14
4 halves, canned, and 2 tablespoons		
heavy syrup	97	27
4 halves, dried	39	10

	Calories	Carbohydrates
Artichokes:*		
1 French or globe, small	50	5½
4 small Jerusalem, frozen	70	4
1 bottom	25	2
Asparagus:		
cooked, cut spears, 1 cup	35	6
6 canned spears, medium	20	3
Avocado:		
California variety, ½ fruit	185	6
Florida variety, ½ fruit	160	11

B

	Calories	Carbohydrates
Bacon:		
½-inch slab (about 2 ounces)	354	0
2 slices	95	1
Bananas, 1 fruit 6 x 1½ inches	85	23
Bean curd:		
1 ounce	20	⅔
½ cup	80	2⅔
Beans:		
green snap, 1 cup	25	6
lima, fresh cooked, 1 cup	180	32
red kidney, ½ cup	290	51
Bean sprouts:		
¼ cup	4	¾
1 tablespoon	1	0
Beef, sirloin lean, 2 ounces	115	0
Beef stock, 1 cup*	22	6
Beet greens, steamed, 1 cup	27	6
Beets:		
cooked, diced, 1 cup	50	12
medium size, 3	50	12
Blackberries, 1 cup	85	19

* Strange are the ways of the artichoke. When stored, its caloric content increases as much as ten times. These listings are therefore approximate.

* Recipe given (see page 39).

	Calories	Carbohydrates
Blueberries, 1 cup	85	21
Bluefish, 3 ounces (raw, flesh only)	100	0
Bone, meal or powdered, ½ teaspoon	0	0
Brains, beef, calf, pork, sheep, 3½ ounces	125	0
Bread:		
cracked wheat, 1 slice	60	12
rye, 1 slice	55	12
whole wheat, 1 slice	55	11
Bread crumbs, dry:		
¼ cup	50	6
1 tablespoon	13	2
Broccoli spears:		
boiled, 1 cup	40	7
steamed, 1 cup	45	8
Brown rice:		
uncooked, 1 ounce	102	22
uncooked, 1 tablespoon	47	10
cooked, 1 tablespoon	35	7½
Brussels sprouts, cooked, 1 cup	45	12
Bulghour, uncooked:		
1 cup	633	132
1 ounce	106	22
Butter (or margarine):		
1 tablespoon (⅛ stick)	100	tr
1 teaspoon	33	tr
1 pat (16 per stick)	50	tr
Buttermilk:		
1 cup	90	13
cultured, 1 cup	127	13

C

	Calories	Carbohydrates
Cabbage, raw:		
finely shredded, 1 cup	25	5
½ head	60	12
Cake, dark fruitcake, 2 x 2 x ½ inches	115	18
Cantaloupe, ½ melon, 5-inch diameter	60	14

	Calories	Carbohydrates
Caraway seeds, ½ teaspoon	0	0
Carrots:		
1 whole, 5½ x 1 inches	20	5
grated, 1 cup	45	11
diced, cooked, 1 cup	45	10
Cashew nuts:		
chopped, 15 nuts, 1 ounce, ¼ cup	150	60
roasted, 1 cup (70 per cup)	760	40
roasted, 1 nut	10	4
roasted, 1 tablespoon	47	1¼
Cauliflower:		
cooked, 1 cup	25	5
uncooked, 1 cup	14	2
Caviar, sturgeon, granular, 1 ounce	74	1
Celery:		
diced, raw, 1 cup	15	4
large stalk, 8 inches	5	2
Chard, steamed, leaves and stalks, 1 cup	30	7
Cheese:		
American, 1-inch cube	70	tr
American, 1 ounce	113	tr
blue, 1 ounce	105	1
camembert, 1 ounce	85	tr
cheddar, 1-inch cube	70	tr
cheddar, grated, 1 tablespoon	30	tr
cheddar, grated, 1 ounce,		
2 tablespoons	60	tr
cottage, from skim milk:		
creamed, 1 cup	240	7
creamed, 1 tablespoon	16	tr
uncreamed, 1 cup	195	6
cream cheese, 1 ounce	105	1
cream cheese, 1 tablespoon	53	tr
cream cheese, 1 teaspoon	18	tr
Cherries, fresh, 1 cup	80	20
Chervil:		
1 tablespoon	2	tr
1 ounce	16	3
Chicken, flesh and skin only:		
1 breast without bone, 8 ounces	160	0
1 breast broiled, 3 ounces	185	0
dark meat, 3 ounces	80	0

	Calories	Carbohydrates
Chicken stock, 1 cup*	2	1
Chili sauce, 1 tablespoon	20	4
Chives:		
1 tablespoon	1	tr
1 ounce	8	1
Clam juice, ¼ cup	12	1
Clams:		
canned, solids and liquids, 3 ounces	45	2
chopped, 1 tablespoon	11	tr
raw, meat only, 3 ounces	65	2
Coconut, dried, shredded:		
1 cup defatted	220	22
1 tablespoon	22	1½
1 teaspoon	8	tr
Coconut meal, unsweetened:		
2 tablespoons, 1 ounce	19	6
¼ cup	38	12
Cod (raw, flesh only), 3 ounces	66	0
Collards, leaves and stalks, 1 cup	51	8
Condensed milk, ¼ cup, sweetened	245	41½
Cookies, plain and assorted, 3-inch		
diameter	120	18
Corn, sweet:		
canned, solids and liquids, 1 cup	170	40
cooked, 5-inch ear	70	16
Cornmeal:		
1 ounce	104	22
1 tablespoon	26	5
Corn oil, 1 tablespoon	125	0
Corn starch:		
1 tablespoon	51	12
1 teaspoon	17	4
1 ounce	102	25
Cottonseed oil, 1 tablespoon	125	0
Couscous (same as Bulghour),		
1 tablespoon	50	11
Crabmeat, canned, 3 ounces	85	1
Crackers:		
graham, plain, 4 small	55	10
whole wheat, 2 pieces, 2-inch square	55	10

* Recipe given (see page 37).

	Calories	Carbohydrates
Cranberry:		
juice, 1 cup	160	41
raw, 1 ounce	12½	3
raw, 1 cup	100	24
sauce, canned, sweetened, 1 cup	405	104
Cream:		
half and half (cream and milk), 1 cup	325	11
half and half, 1 tablespoon	20	1
light whipping, 1 cup	715	9
light whipping, 1 tablespoon	45	1
heavy whipping (volume about double when whipped), 1 cup	840	7
heavy whipping, 1 tablespoon	55	tr
Cucumbers:		
1 raw, 7½ inches long	30	7
6 center slices, ⅛ inch thick	5	2

D

	Calories	Carbohydrates
Dandelion greens:		
boiled, 1 cup	60	12
steamed, 1 cup	80	16
Dates, pitted:		
3 (½ ounce)	15	4
1 cup	490	130
Dill:		
fresh	0	0
dried	0	0
Duck (raw, flesh only), 3 ounces	228	0
Dulse, 1 teaspoon	0	0

E

	Calories	Carbohydrates
Eggplant, raw:		
1 ounce	5	1
½ (4½ ounces)	22	4
Eggs:		
1 large	75	tr
1 white	15	tr
1 yolk	60	tr
Endive, 2 ounces	10	2

F

	Calories	Carbohydrates
Fat, vegetable, for cooking, 1 tablespoon	110	0
Figs, raw:		
fresh, 3 small	90	23
dry, 1 large	60	15
dry, 1 ounce	77	19
Filberts, 10–12	95	3
Finnan haddie (smoked haddock—raw, flesh		
only), 3 ounces	87	0
Flank steak, lean, 1 ounce	40	0
Flounder (raw, flesh only), 3 ounces	66	0
Flour:		
all purpose, 1 cup	400	84
all purpose, 1 tablespoon	25	5
soy, full fat, 1 cup	250	38
whole wheat, 1 cup	400	84

G

	Calories	Carbohydrates
Garlic, 1 clove	½	tr
Gelatin dessert, plain:		
1 cup	140	34
1 tablespoon	9	2
1 teaspoon	3	tr
Ginger root:		
1 tablespoon	6½	1¼
1 slice	1	tr
Goose (raw, flesh only), 3 ounces	221	0
Grapefruit:		
½ white	55	14
½ pink	60	15
sections, canned in syrup, 1 cup	175	44
Grapefruit juice:		
fresh, 1 cup	95	23
canned, sweetened, 1 cup	130	32
Grape juice, canned or bottled, 1 cup	165	42
Grapes:		
American type (Concord), 1 cup	65	15
European type, seedless white, 1 cup	95	25
Green beans, cooked, 1 cup	25	6

	Calories	Carbohydrates
Green pepper:		
large pod	25	5
medium pod	15	3
small pod	10	2
Grouper (raw, flesh only), 3 ounces	75	0
Guinea hen (raw, flesh only), 3 ounces	111	0

H

	Calories	Carbohydrates
Haddock (raw, flesh only), 3 ounces	67	0
Halibut (raw, flesh only), 3 ounces	85	0
Ham:		
3 ounces lean, light cured	245	0
2 ounces boiled	135	0
Hamburger (ground beef), 3 ounces lean	185	0
Heart, beef, lean:		
1 ounce	30	0
1 pound	480	3
Honey:		
1 tablespoon	66	17
1 teaspoon	22	6
raw buckwheat, 1 tablespoon	66	17
Honeydew melon, ¼ melon	50	11
Horseradish:		
1 tablespoon	5	1½
1 teaspoon	1½	½
Horseradish root:		
1 tablespoon	5	1½
1 teaspoon	1½	½

I

	Calories	Carbohydrates
Ice cream, vanilla, organic made with honey, 1 cup	290	26

K

	Calories	Carbohydrates
Kale, steamed, 1 cup	45	8

	Calories	Carbohydrates
Ketchup, tomato:		
1 tablespoon	15	4
1 ounce	30	6
Kidneys, lamb, 3 ounces	87	0
Kohlrabi, raw, sliced, 1 cup	40	9

L

	Calories	Carbohydrates
Lamb:		
1 chop, 4.8 ounces with bone	400	0
cold, 4 slices, 2.5 ounces	130	0
kidneys, 3 ounces	87	0
leg, 2.5 ounces lean	130	0
Lamb quarters, steamed, 1 cup	48	7
Lemon, 1 medium	20	6
Lemon juice, fresh:		
1 cup	80	8
1 tablespoon	4	1
1 teaspoon	1⅓	1
Lentils, uncooked, ½ cup	336	51
Lettuce:		
butterhead (Boston), 1 head, 4-inch diameter	30	6
crisp head (iceberg), 1 head, 4¾-inch diameter	60	13
loose leaf or bunching varieties, 2 large leaves	10	2
Lima beans, dry, 1 ounce	98	18
Lime juice:		
1 cup	65	22
1 tablespoon	4	1
1 teaspoon	1⅓	tr
Liver, calf (raw), 3 ounces	117	4
Liver, chicken:		
3 ounces	108	3
1 ounce	36	1
Lobster, 1 pound	107	1

M

	Calories	Carbohydrates
Mackerel (raw, flesh only), 3 ounces	162	0

	Calories	Carbohydrates
Maple syrup:		
1 tablespoon	36	9
1 ounce	72	18
Mayonnaise, yoghurt, 1 tablespoon*	19	1½
Milk:		
whole, 1 cup	160	12
skim, 1 cup	90	13
evaporated, undiluted, 1 cup	345	24
condensed, sweetened, undiluted,		
1 cup	980	166
dry whole, 1 cup	515	39
goat's, fresh, 1 cup	165	11
skim, instant, 1 cup	216	30
Mint leaves:		
½ teaspoon	0	0
1 tablespoon	1	tr
Miso (soybean paste), 1 tablespoon	24	3½
Molasses:		
light, 1 tablespoon	50	13
blackstrap, 1 tablespoon	45	11
Mung bean sprouts, 1 cup	16	3
Mushrooms:		
canned, 1 cup	40	6
chopped, 1 cup	64	8
1 medium (raw), 2¼-inch diameter	8	1
1 large (raw)	10	1½
Mussels (raw), 3 ounces	81	3
Mustard:		
dry, 3 ounces	0	0
prepared, 1 tablespoon	10	½
Mustard greens, cooked, 1 cup	30	6
Mustard sprouts:		
¼ cup	4	¾
1 tablespoon	1	0

N

Nasturtium leaves (chopped), 1 tablespoon	0	0

* Recipe given (see page 33).

	Calories	Carbohydrates
Nectarines, 2 medium	60	3½
Nutmeg	0	0

O

Oatmeal, cooked:		
1 cup	130	25
1 ounce	55	9
Oats, puffed, 1 ounce	115	21
Oils, all kinds—corn, cottonseed, olive, peanut, safflower, sunflower seed, walnut:		
1 tablespoon	125	0
1 teaspoon	42	0
Olive oil, 1 tablespoon	125	0
Olives:		
green, 3 large	15	tr
ripe, 2 large	15	tr
Onions:		
1 raw, 2½-inch diameter	40	10
chopped, 1 tablespoon	4	1
grated, 1 teaspoon	1	tr
scallion, 1, small with 3-inch green top	4	1
Orange juice, fresh, 1 cup	112	25
Oranges:		
California navel	60	16
Florida	75	19
Oysters, 13–19 medium	160	8

P

Papayas, ½-inch cubes, 1 cup	70	18
Parsley, chopped:		
1 tablespoon	1	tr
1 teaspoon	⅓	0
Parsnips, cooked, 1 cup	100	23
Peaches:		
raw, medium	35	10
nectar, canned, 1 cup	120	31
Peanut butter, organic natural, 1 tablespoon	95	3
Peanut oil, 1 tablespoon	125	0

	Calories	Carbohydrates
Peanuts:		
roasted, 1 cup halves	840	27
chopped, 1 tablespoon	55	2
Pears, raw, medium	100	25
Peas, green:		
cooked, 1 cup	115	19
cooked, 1 tablespoon	7	1
raw, 1 tablespoon	12	2
frozen, 1 tablespoon	10	2
solids and liquids canned, 1 cup	165	31
Pecans:		
halves, 1 cup	740	16
halves, 6 (½ ounce)	98	2
chopped, 1 tablespoon	50	1
Pepper, green, large	25	5
Perch:		
yellow (raw, flesh only), 3 ounces	78	0
white (raw, flesh only), 3 ounces	100	0
Persimmons, Japanese, 1 medium	75	20
Pimiento:		
chopped, 1 tablespoon	4	1
1 medium, canned	10	2
Pineapple:		
fresh diced, 1 cup	75	19
canned, crushed, with syrup, 1 cup	195	50
2 small slices, canned, plus		
2 tablespoons syrup	90	24
Pineapple juice, canned, 1 cup	135	34
Pine nuts:		
1 tablespoon	80	1½
1 ounce	156	3
Pinto beans, uncooked, ½ cup	197	54
Pistachio nuts, 30 nuts	88	3
Plums:		
1 medium, 2-inch diameter	25	7
3 canned, plus 2 tablespoons syrup	100	26
Poppy seeds:		
1 tablespoon	34	0
1 teaspoon	11	0
Pork:		
chop, 3½ ounces	260	0
lean, 2½ ounces	175	0

	Calories	Carbohydrates
Potatoes:		
1 medium (about ⅓ pound) white	90	21
mashed with milk and butter	185	24
1 cup sweet, 6 ounces with shell	155	36
Prune juice, canned, 1 cup	200	49
Prunes, dried, pitted:		
4 medium	70	18
1 cup cooked	300	81
Pumpkin seeds, hulled:		
1 tablespoon	31	1
1 ounce	157	4

R

	Calories	Carbohydrates
Radishes, 4 small	5	1
Raisins, dried:		
1 cup	460	124
1 tablespoon (about 27 raisins)	35	9½
Raspberries:		
black, fresh, 1 cup	100	21
red, fresh, 1 cup	70	17
Red pepper, 1 pod	20	4
Red snapper (raw, flesh only), 3 ounces	79	0
Rhubarb, fresh, diced, 1 cup	19	5
Rice:		
brown, 1 cup	748	154
converted, 1 cup	677	142
flakes, 1 cup	115	26
white, 1 cup	692	150
Rice polish, 3 tablespoons	59	0
Roast beef, lean only, 3 ounces	140	0
Roquefort cheese, 1 ounce	105	1
Rutabagas, diced, 1 cup	42	12
Rye bread, 1 slice	55	12
Rye wafers, 2 wafers, 2 x 3½ inches	45	10

S

	Calories	Carbohydrates
Safflower oil, 1 tablespoon	125	0

	Calories	Carbohydrates
Scallion, 1 small with 3-inch green top	4	1
Sea scallops:		
2 large, 4½ ounces	104	4½
1 ounce	23	1
Sesame seeds:		
1 ounce	160	6
1 tablespoon	40	1½
1 teaspoon	13	½
Shad, 3 ounces	147	0
Shad roe, 3 ounces	148	1½
Shrimp, 1 large (1 ounce)	25	tr
Sirloin beef, lean, 2 ounces	115	0
Snap beans:		
1 cup	25	6
1 tablespoon	2	tr
Sole fillet (raw, flesh only), 3 ounces	78	1
Sour cream:		
2 tablespoons	61	1
1 teaspoon	10	0
Soybean oil, 1 tablespoon	125	0
Soybeans, unseasoned, 1 cup	260	20
Soy sauce:		
1 tablespoon	10	1⅓
1 teaspoon	3	0
Spinach:		
cooked, 1 cup	40	6
canned, 1 cup	45	6
raw chopped, 1 cup	10	1½
frozen chopped, 1 cup	40	6
Sprouts, all varieties—alfalfa, bean, mustard, sprouting wheat, winter wheat:		
¼ cup	4	¾
1 tablespoon	1	0
Squash:		
acorn, ½ of whole	58	16
summer, diced, cooked, 1 cup	30	7
winter, mashed, 1 cup	95	23
Steak:		
lean round, 2.4 ounces	130	0
lean sirloin, 2 ounces	115	0
Strawberries, hulled, 1 cup	55	3

	Calories	Carbohydrates
String beans, raw:		
1 ounce	7	1½
1 cup	25	6
Sturgeon, smoked, 3 ounces	126	0
Sugar, organic raw:		
1 tablespoon	51	3
1 teaspoon	17	1
Sunflower seed oil, 1 tablespoon	125	0
Sunflower seeds, hulled:		
1 tablespoon	79	3
¼ cup	316	12
1 ounce	158	6
Sweetbreads, calf and lamb, 3 ounces	81	0
Sweet potatoes:		
1 medium, about 6 ounces	155	36
canned, 1 cup	235	54
Swiss cheese, 1 ounce	105	1

T

	Calories	Carbohydrates
Tamari:		
1 tablespoon	10	1⅓
1 teaspoon	3	0
Tangerines, raw, 1 medium	40	10
Tapioca, quick-cooking, dry, 1 tablespoon	35	9
Tarragon leaves	0	0
Tea, without sugar, milk or lemon, 1 cup	0	0
Tiger's Milk powder:		
vanilla, ⅓ cup	124	21
carob flavor, 2 tablespoons	124	7
Tomatoes:		
raw, 1 large	50	9
raw, 1 medium	35	7
raw, 1 cherry tomato	5	½
raw, 1 shell	18	3½
Tomato juice, canned, 1 cup	45	10
Tomato ketchup, 1 tablespoon	15	4
Tomato purée, 1 ounce	11	2½
Tongue, beef, braised, 3 ounces	210	tr
Trout, rainbow, 3 ounces	168	0
Tuna (raw, flesh only), 3 ounces	123	0

	Calories	Carbohydrates
Turkey, fat mature bird, raw,		
3 ounces	294	0
Turnips:		
cooked, diced, 1 cup	35	8
greens, steamed, 1 cup	45	8

V

	Calories	Carbohydrates
Vanilla bean	0	0
Veal:		
loin chop without tail, 6 ounces	264	0
lean cut for scallopini, 3 ounces	185	0
Vegetable stock, 1 cup*	81	25
Vinegar:		
cider, 1 tablespoon	2	1
cider, 1 teaspoon	1⅓	0
cider, 1 cup	32	16
tarragon, 1 tablespoon	2	1
tarragon, 1 teaspoon	⅔	0

W

	Calories	Carbohydrates
Walnuts, shelled:		
black, 1 cup	790	19
English, 1 cup	650	16
English, 16 quarters (1 ounce)	178	2
Water chestnuts, 1 medium-sized	6	1
Watercress, 1 cup	4	tr
Watermelon, raw, 4 x 8-inch wedge	115	27
Wheat sprouts:		
¼ cup	4	¾
1 tablespoon	1	0
Wheat, unground, cooked, 1 cup	344	44
Wheat flakes:		
1 tablespoon	50	11
1 ounce	100	23
Wheat germ:		
1 tablespoon	15	2
1 teaspoon	5	½
1 cup	245	34

* Recipe given (see page 38).

	Calories	Carbohydrates
Wheat meal cereal, uncooked, 1 cup	412	100
Whole wheat bread, 1 slice	55	11
Whole wheat flour:		
1 tablespoon	25	5
1 teaspoon	8	1½
1 cup	400	84

Y

	Calories	Carbohydrates
Yeast:		
nutritional, 1 teaspoon	7	3
dry active, 1 tablespoon	13	2
Yoghurt, from partially skimmed milk:		
1 cup	120	13
1 tablespoon	8	1
1 teaspoon	3	0
1 ounce	15	2

Z

	Calories	Carbohydrates
Zucchini:		
1 cup	46	8
1 ounce	6	1

Food	Quantity	Pro-tein grams	Carbo-hydrate grams	Fat grams	Satu-rated fatty acids grams
FRUITS					
Apple juice	1 cup	tr	30	tr	—
Apples, raw	1 med.	tr	18	tr	—
Applesauce, canned:					
Sweetened	1 cup	1	61	tr	—
Unsweetened	1 cup	1	26	tr	—
Apricot nectar, canned	1 cup	1	37	tr	—
Apricots:					
Raw	3 med.	1	14	tr	—
Canned in heavy syrup	1 cup	2	57	tr	—
Dried, uncooked	1 cup	8	100	1	—
Cooked	1 cup	5	62	1	—
Avocados:					
California	1	5	13	37	7
Florida	1	4	27	33	7
Banana flakes	1 cup	4	89	1	—
Bananas, raw	1 med.	1	26	tr	—
Blackberries, raw	1 cup	2	19	1	—
Blueberries, raw	1 cup	1	21	1	—
Cantaloups, raw	½ med.	1	14	tr	—
Cherries, canned, water					
pack	1 cup	2	26	tr	—
Cranberry juice	1 cup	tr	42	tr	—
Cranberry sauce	1 cup	tr	85	1	—
Dates, pitted, cut	1 cup	4	130	1	—
Figs, dried	1 large	1	15	tr	—
Fruit cocktail, canned					
in heavy syrup	1 cup	1	50	tr	—
Grapefruit:					
Raw					
White	½ med.	1	12	tr	—
Pink or red	½ med.	1	13	tr	—
Canned, syrup pack	1 cup	2	45	tr	—
Grapefruit juice:					
Fresh	1 cup	1	23	tr	—
Canned					
Unsweetened	1 cup	1	24	tr	—
Sweetened	1 cup	1	32	tr	—
Frozen, concentrate,					
unsweetened:					
Undiluted	6-oz. can	4	72	1	—
Diluted	1 cup	1	24	tr	—

SOURCE: U.S. Department of Agriculture, *Home and Garden Bulletin* No. 72

Lino-leic acid grams	Cal-cium mg.	Iron mg.	Vitamins A units	B₁ mg.	B₂ mg.	Niacin mg.	C mg.
—	15	1.5	—	.02	.05	.2	2
—	8	.4	50	.04	.02	.1	3
—	10	1.3	100	.05	.03	.1	3
—	10	1.2	100	.05	.02	.1	2
—	23	.5	2,380	.03	.03	.5	8
—	18	.5	2,890	.03	.04	.7	10
—	28	.8	4,510	.05	.06	.9	10
—	100	8.2	16,350	.02	.23	4.9	19
—	63	5.1	8,550	.01	.13	2.8	8
5	22	1.3	630	.24	.43	3.5	30
4	30	1.8	880	.33	.61	4.9	43
—	32	2.8	760	.18	.24	2.8	7
—	10	.8	230	.06	.07	.8	12
—	46	1.3	290	.05	.06	.5	30
—	21	1.4	140	.04	.08	.6	20
—	27	.8	6,540	.08	.06	1.2	63
—	37	.7	1,660	.07	.05	.5	12
—	13	.8	tr	.03	.03	.1	40
—	14	.5	50	.02	.02	.1	5
—	105	5.3	90	.16	.17	3.9	0
—	26	.6	20	.02	.02	.1	0
—	23	1.0	360	.05	.03	1.3	5
—	19	.5	10	.05	.02	.2	44
—	20	.5	540	.05	.02	.2	44
—	33	.8	30	.08	.05	.5	76
—	22	.5	—	.09	.04	.4	92
—	20	1.0	20	.07	.04	.4	84
—	20	1.0	20	.07	.04	.4	78
—	70	.8	60	.29	.12	1.4	286
—	25	.2	20	.10	.04	.5	96

tr = trace   — = lack of reliable data

Food	Quantity	Pro-tein grams	Carbo-hydrate grams	Fat grams	Satu-rated fatty acids grams
Grapejuice:					
Canned or bottled	1 cup	1	42	tr	—
Frozen concentrate, sweetened:					
Undiluted	6-oz. can	1	100	tr	—
Diluted	1 cup	1	33	tr	—
Grapes, raw:					
American	1 cup	1	15	1	—
European	1 cup	1	25	tr	—
Lemon juice	1 cup	1	20	tr	—
Lemons, raw	1 med.	1	6	tr	—
Lime juice:					
Fresh	1 cup	1	22	tr	—
Canned, unsweetened	1 cup	1	22	tr	—
Orange juice, fresh	1 cup	2	26	1	—
Canned, unsweetened	1 cup	2	28	tr	—
Frozen, concentrate:					
Undiluted	6-oz. can	5	87	tr	—
Diluted	1 cup	2	29	tr	—
Orange and grapefruit juice:					
Frozen concentrate:					
Undiluted	6-oz. can	4	78	1	—
Diluted	1 cup	1	26	tr	—
Oranges, raw	1 med.	1	16	tr	—
Papayas, raw	1 cup	1	18	tr	—
Peaches:					
Raw:					
Whole	1 med.	1	10	tr	—
Sliced	1 cup	1	16	tr	—
Canned:					
Syrup pack	1 cup	1	52	tr	—
Water pack	1 cup	1	20	tr	—
Dried, uncooked	1 cup	5	109	1	—
Cooked	1 cup	3	58	1	—
Frozen	12-oz. box	1	77	tr	—
Pears:					
Raw	1 med.	1	25	1	—
Canned, syrup pack	1 cup	1	50	1	—
Pineapple:					
Raw, diced	1 cup	1	19	tr	—
Canned, heavy syrup:					
Crushed	1 cup	1	50	tr	—
Sliced	2 small	tr	24	tr	—

Lino- leic acid grams	Cal- cium mg.	Iron mg.	Vitamins A units	B₁ mg.	B₂ mg.	Niacin mg.	C mg.
—	28	.8	—	.10	.05	.5	tr
—	22	.9	40	.13	.22	1.5	—
—	8	.3	10	.05	.08	.5	—
—	15	.4	100	.05	.03	.2	3
—	17	.6	140	.07	.04	.4	6
—	17	.5	50	.07	.02	.2	112
—	19	.4	10	.03	.01	.1	39
—	22	.5	20	.05	.02	.2	79
—	22	.5	20	.05	.02	.2	52
—	27	.5	500	.22	.07	1.0	124
—	25	1.0	500	.17	.05	.7	100
—	75	.9	1,620	.68	.11	2.8	360
—	25	.2	550	.22	.02	1.0	120
—	61	.8	800	.48	.06	2.3	302
—	20	.2	270	.16	.02	.8	102
—	54	.5	260	.13	.05	.5	66
—	36	.5	3,190	.07	.08	.5	102
—	9	.5	1,320	.02	.05	1.0	7
—	15	.8	2,230	.03	.08	1.6	12
—	10	.8	1,100	.02	.06	1.4	7
—	10	.7	1,100	.02	.06	1.4	7
—	77	9.6	6,240	.02	.31	8.5	28
—	41	5.1	3,290	.01	.15	4.2	6
—	14	1.7	2,210	.03	.14	2.4	135
—	13	.5	30	.04	.07	.2	7
—	13	.5	tr	.03	.05	.3	4
—	24	.7	100	.12	.04	.3	24
—	29	.8	120	.20	.06	.5	17
—	13	.4	50	.09	.03	.2	8

tr = trace   — = lack of reliable data

Food	Quantity	Pro-tein grams	Carbo-hydrate grams	Fat grams	Satu-rated fatty acids grams
Pineapple juice, canned	1 cup	1	34	tr	—
Plums:					
Raw	1 med.	tr	7	tr	—
Canned, syrup pack	1 cup	1	53	tr	—
Prune juice	1 cup	1	49	tr	—
Prunes, dried					
Uncooked	4 med.	1	18	tr	—
Cooked	1 cup	2	78	1	—
Raisins, seedless	1 cup	4	128	tr	—
Raspberries, red:					
Raw	1 cup	1	17	1	—
Frozen	10-oz. box	2	70	1	—
Rhubarb, cooked, sweetened	1 cup	1	98	tr	—
Strawberries:					
Raw	1 cup	1	13	1	—
Frozen	10-oz. box	1	79	1	—
Tangerine juice, sweetened	1 cup	1	30	1	—
Tangerines, raw	1 med.	1	10	tr	—
Watermelon, raw	1 wedge	2	27	1	—

VEGETABLES

Food	Quantity	Pro-tein grams	Carbo-hydrate grams	Fat grams	Satu-rated fatty acids grams
Asparagus, green, cooked	4 spears	1	2	tr	—
Pieces	1 cup	3	5	tr	—
Canned	1 cup	5	7	1	—
Beans:					
Dry:					
Great Northern	1 cup	14	38	1	—
Lima, cooked, drained	1 cup	16	49	1	—
Navy (pea)	1 cup	15	40	1	—
Green:					
Canned	1 cup	2	10	tr	—
Cooked	1 cup	2	7	tr	—
Lima, cooked, drained	1 cup	13	34	1	—
Mung, sprouted, cooked, drained	1 cup	4	7	tr	—
Red kidney, canned	1 cup	15	42	1	—
Wax:					
Canned	1 cup	2	10	1	—
Cooked	1 cup	2	6	tr	—
Beet greens	1 cup	3	5	tr	—

Lino-leic acid grams	Cal-cium mg.	Iron mg.	Vitamins A units	B₁ mg.	B₂ mg.	Niacin mg.	C mg.
—	37	.7	120	.12	.04	.5	22
—	7	.3	140	.02	.02	.3	3
—	22	2.2	2,970	.05	.05	.9	4
—	36	10.5	—	.03	.03	1.0	5
—	14	1.1	440	.02	.04	.4	1
—	60	4.5	1,860	.08	.18	1.7	2
—	102	.58	30	.18	.13	.8	2
—	27	1.1	160	.04	.11	1.1	31
—	37	1.7	200	.06	.17	1.7	59
—	212	1.6	220	.06	.15	.7	17
—	31	1.5	90	.04	.10	1.0	88
—	40	2.0	90	.06	.17	1.5	150
—	45	.5	1,050	.15	.05	.2	55
—	34	.3	360	.05	.02	.1	27
—	30	2.1	2,510	.13	.13	.7	30
—	13	.4	540	.10	.11	.8	16
—	30	.9	1,310	.23	.26	2.0	38
—	44	4.1	1,240	.15	.22	2.0	37
—	90	4.9	0	.25	.13	1.3	0
—	55	5.9	—	.25	.11	1.3	—
—	95	5.1	0	.27	.13	1.3	0
—	81	2.9	690	.07	.10	.7	10
—	63	.8	680	.09	.11	.6	15
—	80	4.3	480	.31	.17	2.2	29
—	21	1.1	30	.11	.13	.9	8
—	74	4.6	10	.13	.10	1.5	—
—	81	2.9	140	.07	.10	.7	12
—	63	.8	290	.09	.11	.6	16
—	144	2.8	7,400	.10	.22	.4	22

tr = trace   — = lack of reliable data

Food	Quantity	Pro-tein grams	Carbo-hydrate grams	Fat grams	Satu-rated fatty acids grams
Beets:					
Cooked, drained:					
Whole	2 med.	1	7	tr	—
Diced	1 cup	2	12	tr	—
Canned	1 cup	2	19	tr	—
Broccoli, cooked:					
Whole	1 med. stalk	6	8	1	—
Cut pieces	1 cup	5	7	1	—
Chopped	1⅜ cups	7	12	1	—
Brussels sprouts	1 cup	7	10	1	—
Cabbage:					
Raw:					
Coarsely shredded	1 cup	1	4	tr	—
Finely shredded	1 cup	1	5	tr	—
Cooked	1 cup	2	6	tr	—
Red, raw, coarsely shredded	1 cup	1	5	tr	—
Cabbage, Chinese, raw	1 cup	1	2	tr	—
Carrots:					
Raw:					
Whole	1	1	5	tr	—
Grated	1 cup	1	11	tr	—
Canned	1 oz.	tr	2	tr	—
Cooked	1 cup	1	10	tr	—
Cauliflower, cooked	1 cup	3	5	tr	—
Celery, raw:					
Stalk	1	tr	2	tr	—
Pieces	1 cup	1	4	tr	—
Collards, cooked	1 cup	5	9	1	—
Corn, sweet:					
Ear	1	3	16	1	—
Canned	1 cup	5	40	2	—
Cucumbers, raw:					
Pared	1	1	7	tr	—
Sliced	6 slices	tr	2	tr	—
Dandelion greens, cooked	1 cup	4	12	1	—
Endive and escarole	2 oz.	1	2	tr	—
Kale, cooked	1 cup	4	4	1	—
Lettuce, raw:					
Boston	1 head	3	6	tr	—
Iceberg	1 head	4	13	tr	—
Looseleaf	2 large leaves	1	2	tr	—
Mushrooms, canned	1 cup	5	6	tr	—

Lino-leic acid grams	Cal-cium mg.	Iron mg.	Vitamins				
			A units	B$_1$ mg.	B$_2$ mg.	Niacin mg.	C mg.
—	14	.5	20	.03	.04	.3	6
—	24	.9	30	.05	.07	.5	10
—	34	1.5	20	.02	.05	.2	7
—	158	1.4	4,500	.16	.36	1.4	162
—	136	1.2	3,880	.14	.31	1.2	140
—	135	1.8	6,500	.15	.30	1.3	143
—	50	1.7	810	.12	.22	1.2	135
—	34	.3	90	.04	.04	.2	33
—	44	.4	120	.05	.05	.3	42
—	64	.4	190	.06	.06	.4	48
—	29	.6	30	.06	.04	.3	43
—	32	.5	110	.04	.03	.5	19
—	18	.4	5,500	.03	.03	.3	4
—	41	.8	12,100	.06	.06	.7	9
—	7	.1	3,690	.01	.01	.1	1
—	48	.9	15,220	.08	.07	.7	9
—	25	.8	70	.11	.10	.7	66
—	16	.1	100	.01	.01	.1	4
—	39	.3	240	.03	.03	.3	9
—	289	1.1	10,260	.27	.37	2.4	87
—	2	.5	310	.09	.08	1.0	7
—	10	1.0	690	.07	.12	2.3	13
—	35	.6	tr	.07	.09	.4	23
—	8	.2	tr	.02	.02	.1	6
—	252	3.2	21,060	.24	.29	—	32
—	46	1.0	1,870	.04	.08	.3	6
—	147	1.3	8,140	—	—	—	68
—	77	4.4	2,130	.14	.13	.6	18
—	91	2.3	1,500	.29	.27	1.3	29
—	34	.7	950	.03	.04	.2	9
—	15	1.2	tr	.04	.60	4.8	4

tr = trace   — = lack of reliable data

Food	Quantity	Pro-tein grams	Carbo-hydrate grams	Fat grams	Satu-rated fatty acids grams
Mustard greens, cooked	1 cup	3	6	1	—
Okra, cooked	8 pods	2	5	tr	—
Onions:					
Mature:					
Raw	1 med.	2	10	tr	—
Cooked	1 cup	3	14	tr	—
Green:	6	1	5	tr	—
Parsley, raw	1 tb.	tr	tr	tr	—
Parsnips, cooked	1 cup	2	23	1	—
Peas:					
Blackeye, dry, cooked	1 cup	13	34	1	—
Green:					
Canned	1 cup	9	31	1	—
Cooked	1 cup	9	19	1	—
Split, dry, cooked	1 cup	20	52	1	—
Peppers, hot, red	1 tb.	2	8	2	—
Peppers, sweet:					
Raw, green	1	1	4	tr	—
Cooked	1	1	3	tr	—
Potato chips	10 med.	1	10	8	2
Potatoes:					
Baked	1 med.	3	21	tr	—
Boiled, peeled	1 potato	3	23	tr	—
French-fried	10 pieces	2	20	7	2
Mashed with milk	1 cup	4	25	1	—
Pumpkin, canned	1 cup	2	18	1	—
Radishes	4 small	tr	1	tr	—
Sauerkraut, canned	1 cup	2	9	tr	—
Spinach:					
Canned	1 cup	5	6	1	—
Cooked	1 cup	5	6	1	—
Squash:					
Cooked:					
Summer	1 cup	2	7	tr	—
Winter, mashed	1 cup	4	32	1	—
Sweet potatoes:					
Baked	1 med.	2	36	1	—
Boiled	1 med.	2	39	1	—
Candied	1 med.	2	60	6	2
Canned	1 cup	4	54	tr	—
Tomatoes:					
Raw	1 med.	2	9	tr	—
Canned	1 cup	2	10	1	—
Tomato juice, canned	1 cup	2	10	tr	—

Lino-leic acid grams	Cal-cium mg.	Iron mg.	Vitamins				
			A units	B₁ mg.	B₂ mg.	Niacin mg.	C mg.
—	193	2.5	8,120	.11	.19	.9	68
—	78	.4	420	.11	.15	.8	17
—	30	.6	40	.04	.04	.2	11
—	50	.8	80	.06	.06	.4	14
—	20	.3	tr	.02	.02	.2	12
—	8	.2	340	tr	.01	tr	7
—	70	.9	50	.11	.12	.2	16
—	42	3.2	20	.41	.11	1.1	tr
—	50	4.2	1,120	.23	.13	2.2	22
—	37	2.9	860	.44	.17	3.7	33
—	28	4.2	100	.37	.22	2.2	—
—	40	2.3	9,750	.03	.17	1.3	2
—	7	.5	310	.06	.06	.4	94
—	7	.4	310	.05	.05	.4	70
4	8	.4	tr	.04	.01	1.0	3
—	9	.7	tr	.10	.04	1.7	20
—	10	.8	tr	.13	.05	2.0	22
4	9	.7	tr	.07	.04	1.8	12
—	47	.8	50	.16	.10	2.0	19
—	57	.9	14,590	.07	.12	1.3	12
—	12	.4	tr	.01	.01	.1	10
—	85	1.2	120	.07	.09	.4	33
—	212	4.7	14,400	.03	.21	.6	24
—	167	4.0	14,580	.13	.25	1.0	50
—	52	.8	820	.10	.16	1.6	21
—	57	1.6	8,610	.10	.27	1.4	27
—	44	1.0	8,910	.10	.07	.7	24
—	47	1.0	11,610	.13	.09	.9	25
1	65	1.6	11,030	.10	.08	.8	17
—	54	1.7	17,000	.10	.10	1.4	30
—	24	.9	1,640	.11	.07	1.3	42
—	14	1.2	2,170	.12	.07	1.7	41
—	17	2.2	1,940	.12	.07	1.9	39

tr = trace   — = lack of reliable data

Food	Quantity	Pro-tein grams	Carbo-hydrate grams	Fat grams	Satu-rated fatty acids grams
Turnip greens, cooked	1 cup	3	5	tr	—
Turnips, cooked	1 cup	1	8	tr	—
MEAT AND POULTRY					
Bacon, cooked	2 slices	5	1	8	3
Beef, canned:					
Corned beef	3 oz.	22	0	10	5
Corned beef hash	3 oz.	7	9	10	5
Beef, chipped	2 oz.	19	0	4	2
Beef, cooked:					
Braised:					
Lean and fat	3 oz.	23	0	16	8
Lean only	2.5 oz.	22	0	5	2
Hamburger, broiled:					
Lean	3 oz.	23	0	10	5
Regular	3 oz.	21	0	17	8
Roast:					
Rib:					
Lean and fat	3 oz.	17	0	34	16
Lean only	1.8 oz.	14	0	7	3
Round:					
Lean and fat	3 oz.	25	0	7	3
Lean only	2.7 oz.	24	0	3	1
Steak, broiled:					
Sirloin:					
Lean and fat	3 oz.	20	0	27	13
Lean only	2 oz.	18	0	4	2
Round:					
Lean and fat	3 oz.	24	0	13	6
Lean only	2.4 oz.	21	0	4	2
Chicken, canned, boneless	3 oz.	18	0	10	3
Chicken, cooked:					
Flesh only, broiled	3 oz.	20	0	3	1
Breast, fried:					
With bone	3.3 oz.	25	1	5	1
Flesh and skin only	2.7 oz.	25	1	5	1
Drumstick, fried:					
With bone	2.1 oz.	12	tr	4	1
Flesh and skin only	1.3 oz.	12	tr	4	1
Heart, beef, braised	3 oz.	27	1	5	—
Lamb, cooked:					
Chop	4.8 oz.	25	0	33	18
Lean and fat	4.0 oz.	25	0	33	18

Lino-leic acid grams	Cal-cium mg.	Iron mg.	Vitamins				
			A units	B₁ mg.	B₂ mg.	Niacin mg.	C mg.
—	252	1.5	8,270	.15	.33	.7	68
—	54	.6	tr	.06	.08	.5	34
1	2	.5	0	.08	.05	.8	—
tr	17	3.7	20	.01	.20	2.9	—
tr	11	1.7	—	.01	.08	1.8	—
tr	11	2.9	—	.04	.18	2.2	—
tr	10	2.9	30	.04	.18	3.5	—
tr	10	2.7	10	.04	.16	3.3	—
tr	10	3.0	20	.08	.20	5.1	—
tr	9	2.7	30	.07	.18	4.6	—
1	8	2.2	70	.05	.13	3.1	—
tr	6	1.8	10	.04	.11	2.6	—
tr	11	3.2	10	.06	.19	4.5	—
tr	10	3.0	tr	.06	.18	4.3	—
1	9	2.5	50	.05	.16	4.0	—
tr	7	2.2	10	.05	.14	3.6	—
tr	10	3.0	20	.07	.19	4.8	—
tr	9	2.5	10	.06	.16	4.1	—
2	18	1.3	200	.03	.11	3.7	3
1	8	1.4	80	.05	.16	7.4	—
1	9	1.3	70	.04	.17	11.2	—
1	9	1.3	70	.04	.17	11.2	—
1	6	.9	50	.03	.15	2.7	—
1	6	.9	50	.03	.15	2.7	—
—	5	5.0	20	.21	1.04	6.5	1
1	10	1.5	—	.14	.25	5.6	—
1	10	1.5	—	.14	.25	5.6	—

tr = trace   — = lack of reliable data

Food	Quantity	Pro-tein grams	Carbo-hydrate grams	Fat grams	Satu-rated fatty acids grams
Lamb (cont.)					
Lean only	2.6 oz.	21	0	6	3
Leg, roasted:					
Lean and fat	3 oz.	22	0	16	9
Lean only	2.5 oz.	20	0	5	3
Shoulder, roasted:					
Lean and fat	3 oz.	18	0	23	13
Lean only	2.3 oz.	17	0	6	3
Liver, beef, fried	2 oz.	15	3	6	—
Pork, cured, cooked:					
Ham	3 oz.	18	0	19	7
Luncheon meat:					
Boiled ham	2 oz.	11	0	10	4
Canned	2 oz.	8	1	14	5
Pork, fresh, cooked:					
Chop	3.5 oz.	16	0	21	8
Lean and fat	2.3 oz.	16	0	21	8
Lean only	1.7 oz.	15	0	7	2
Roast:					
Lean and fat	3 oz.	21	0	24	9
Lean only	2.4 oz.	20	0	10	3
Simmered:					
Lean and fat	3 oz.	20	0	26	9
Lean only	2.2 oz.	18	0	6	2
Sausage:					
Bologna	2 slices	3	tr	7	—
Braunschweiger	2 slices	3	tr	5	—
Deviled ham, canned	1 tb.	2	0	4	2
Frankfurter	1	7	1	15	—
Pork links, cooked	2	5	tr	11	4
Salami, cooked	1 oz.	5	tr	7	—
Salami, dry	1 oz.	7	tr	11	—
Vienna, canned	1	2	tr	3	—
Veal, cooked, without bone:					
Cutlet	3 oz.	23	—	9	5
Roast	3 oz.	23	0	14	7
FISH AND SEAFOOD					
Bluefish, baked	3 oz.	22	0	4	—
Clams:					
Raw	3 oz.	11	2	1	—
Canned	3 oz.	7	2	1	—
Crabmeat, canned	3 oz.	15	1	2	—
Haddock, breaded, fried	3 oz.	17	5	5	1

Lino-leic acid grams	Cal-cium mg.	Iron mg.	Vitamins				
			A units	B₁ mg.	B₂ mg.	Niacin mg.	C mg.
tr	9	1.5	—	.11	.20	4.5	—
tr	9	1.4	—	.13	.23	4.7	—
tr	9	1.4	—	.12	.21	4.4	—
1	9	1.0	—	.11	.20	4.0	—
tr	8	1.0	—	.10	.18	3.7	—
—	6	5.0	30,280	.15	2.37	9.4	15
2	8	2.2	0	.40	.16	3.1	—
1	6	1.6	0	.25	.09	1.5	—
1	5	1.2	0	.18	.12	1.6	—
2	8	2.2	0	.63	.18	3.8	—
2	8	2.2	0	.63	.18	3.8	—
1	7	1.9	0	.54	.16	3.3	—
2	9	2.7	0	.78	.22	4.7	—
1	9	2.6	0	.73	.21	4.4	—
2	8	2.5	0	.46	.21	4.1	—
1	8	2.3	0	.42	.19	3.7	—
—	2	.5	—	.04	.06	.7	—
—	2	1.2	1,310	.03	.29	1.6	—
tr	1	.3	—	.02	.01	.2	—
—	3	.8	—	.08	.11	1.4	—
1	2	.6	0	.21	.09	1.0	—
—	3	.7	—	.07	.07	1.2	—
—	4	1.0	—	.10	.07	1.5	—
—	1	.3	—	.01	.02	.4	—
tr	9	2.7	—	.06	.21	4.6	—
tr	10	2.9	—	.11	.26	6.6	—
—	25	.6	40	.09	.08	1.6	—
—	59	5.2	90	.08	.15	1.1	8
—	47	3.5	—	.01	.09	.9	—
—	38	.7	—	.07	.07	1.6	—
tr	34	1.0	—	.03	.06	2.7	2

tr = trace   — = lack of reliable data

Food	Quantity	Pro-tein grams	Carbo-hydrate grams	Fat grams	Satu-rated fatty acids grams
Ocean perch, breaded, fried	3 oz.	16	6	11	—
Oysters, raw	1 cup	20	8	4	—
Salmon, pink, canned	3 oz.	17	0	5	1
Sardines, canned in oil	3 oz.	20	0	9	—
Shad, baked	3 oz.	20	0	10	—
Shrimp, canned	3 oz.	21	1	1	—
Swordfish, broiled	3 oz.	24	0	5	—
Tuna, canned in oil	3 oz.	24	0	7	2
DAIRY PRODUCTS					
Buttermilk	1 cup	9	12	tr	—
Cheese:					
Blue or Roquefort	1 oz.	6	1	9	5
	1 cu. in.	4	tr	5	3
Camembert	1 wedge	7	1	9	5
Cheddar	1 oz.	7	1	9	5
	1 cu. in.	4	tr	6	3
Cottage:					
Creamed	1 cup	33	7	10	6
Uncreamed	1 cup	34	5	1	tr
Cream	1 8-oz. pkg.	18	5	86	48
	1 3-oz. pkg.	7	2	32	18
	1 cu. in.	1	tr	6	3
Parmesan, grated	1 cup	60	5	43	24
	1 oz.	12	1	9	5
Swiss	1 oz.	8	1	8	4
	1 cu. in.	4	tr	4	2
Cream:					
Half-and-half	1 cup	8	11	28	15
	1 tb.	1	1	2	1
Light	1 cup	7	10	49	27
	1 tb.	1	1	3	2
Sour	1 cup	7	10	47	26
	1 tb.	tr	1	2	1
Whipping:					
Light	1 cup	6	9	75	41
	1 tb.	tr	1	5	3
Heavy	1 cup	5	7	90	50
	1 tb.	tr	1	6	3
Eggs:					
Whole	1 large	6	tr	6	2
White	1	4	tr	tr	—
Yolk	1	3	tr	5	2
Scrambled with milk	1 egg	7	1	8	3

Lino- leic acid grams	Cal- cium mg.	Iron mg.	Vitamins				
			A units	B$_1$ mg.	B$_2$ mg.	Niacin mg.	C mg.
—	28	1.1	—	.08	.09	1.5	—
—	226	13.2	740	.33	.43	6.0	—
tr	167	.7	60	.03	.16	6.8	—
—	372	2.5	190	.02	.17	4.6	—
—	20	.5	20	.11	.22	7.3	—
—	98	2.6	50	.01	.03	1.5	—
—	23	1.1	1,750	.03	.04	9.3	—
1	7	1.6	70	.04	.10	10.1	—
—	296	.1	10	.10	.44	.2	2
tr	89	.1	350	.01	.17	.3	0
tr	54	.1	210	.01	.11	.2	0
tr	40	.2	380	.02	.29	.3	0
tr	213	.3	370	.01	.13	tr	0
tr	129	.2	230	.01	.08	tr	0
tr	230	.7	420	.07	.61	.2	0
tr	180	.8	20	.06	.56	.2	0
3	141	.5	3,500	.05	.54	.2	0
1	53	.2	1,310	.02	.20	.1	0
tr	10	tr	250	tr	.04	tr	0
1	1,893	.7	1,760	.03	1.22	.3	0
tr	383	.1	360	.01	.25	.1	0
tr	262	.3	320	tr	.11	tr	0
tr	139	.1	170	tr	.06	tr	0
1	261	.1	1,160	.07	.39	.1	2
tr	16	tr	70	tr	.02	tr	tr
1	245	.1	2,020	.07	.36	.1	2
tr	15	tr	130	tr	.02	tr	tr
1	235	.1	1,930	.07	.35	.1	2
tr	12	tr	100	tr	.02	tr	tr
2	203	.1	3,060	.05	.29	.1	2
tr	13	tr	190	tr	.02	tr	tr
3	179	.1	3,670	.05	.26	.1	2
tr	11	tr	230	tr	.02	tr	tr
tr	27	1.1	590	.05	.15	tr	0
—	3	tr	0	tr	.09	tr	0
tr	24	.9	580	.04	.07	tr	0
tr	51	1.1	690	.05	.18	tr	0

tr = trace   — = lack of reliable data

Food	Quantity	Pro-tein grams	Carbo-hydrate grams	Fat grams	Satu-rated fatty acids grams
Milk:					
Fluid:					
Whole	1 cup	9	12	9	5
Skim	1 cup	9	12	tr	—
Canned, evaporated,					
undiluted	1 cup	18	24	20	11
Dry, nonfat:					
Instant	1 cup	24	35	tr	—
Non-instant	1 cup	37	54	1	—
Yoghurt:					
From partially					
skimmed milk	1 cup	8	13	4	2
From whole milk	1 cup	7	12	8	5
OILS AND FATS					
Butter	½ cup	1	1	92	51
	1 tb.	tr	tr	12	6
	1 pat	tr	tr	4	2
Fats, cooking:					
Lard	1 cup	0	0	205	78
	1 tb.	0	0	13	5
Vegetable fats	1 cup	0	0	200	50
	1 tb.	0	0	13	3
Margarine:	½ cup	1	1	92	17
	1 tb.	tr	tr	12	2
	1 pat	tr	tr	4	1
Oils, salad or cooking	1 cup	0	0	220	22
	1 tb.	0	0	14	1
Salad dressings:					
Blue cheese	1 tb.	1	1	8	2
French	1 tb.	tr	3	6	1
Home cooked, boiled	1 tb.	1	2	2	1
Mayonnaise	1 tb.	tr	tr	11	2
Thousand island	1 tb.	tr	3	8	1
BREAD AND GRAIN PRODUCTS					
Bran flakes	1 cup	4	28	1	—
Bread:					
Cracked wheat	1 slice	2	13	1	—
Rye, light	1 slice	2	13	tr	—
Whole wheat	1-lb. loaf	41	224	12	2
	1 slice	3	14	1	—
Bulghour, canned	1 cup	8	44	4	—

Lino-leic acid grams	Cal-cium mg.	Iron mg.	Vitamins				
			A units	B$_1$ mg.	B$_2$ mg.	Niacin mg.	C mg.
tr	288	.1	350	.07	.41	.2	2
—	296	.1	10	.09	.44	.2	2
1	635	.3	810	.10	.86	.5	3
—	879	.4	20	.24	1.21	.6	5
—	1,345	.6	30	.36	1.85	.9	7
tr	294	.1	170	.10	.44	.2	2
tr	272	.1	340	.07	.39	.2	2
3	23	0	3,750	—	—	—	0
tr	3	0	470	—	—	—	0
tr	1	0	170	—	—	—	0
20	0	0	0	0	0	0	0
1	0	0	0	0	0	0	0
44	0	0	—	0	0	0	0
3	0	0	—	0	0	0	0
25	23	0	3,750	—	—	—	0
3	3	0	470	—	—	—	0
1	1	0	170	—	—	—	0
117	0	0	—	0	0	0	0
7	0	0	—	0	0	0	0
4	12	tr	30	tr	.02	tr	tr
3	2	.1	—	—	—	—	—
tr	14	.1	80	.01	.03	tr	tr
6	3	.1	40	tr	.01	tr	—
4	2	.1	50	tr	tr	tr	tr
—	25	12.3	0	.14	.06	2.2	0
—	22	.3	tr	.03	.02	.3	tr
—	19	.4	0	.05	.02	.4	0
2	381	13.6	tr	1.36	.45	12.7	tr
—	24	.8	tr	.09	.03	.8	tr
—	27	1.9	0	.08	.05	4.1	0

tr = trace   — = lack of reliable data

307

Food	Quantity	Pro-tein grams	Carbo-hydrate grams	Fat grams	Satu-rated fatty acids grams
Corn grits, yellow, cooked	1 cup	3	27	tr	—
Cornmeal, yellow	1 cup	11	90	5	1
Farina, enriched, cooked	1 cup	3	22	tr	—
Flour:					
Soy, full fat	1 cup	39	33	22	0
Wheat, all purpose, sifted	1 cup	12	88	1	—
Whole wheat	1 cup	16	85	2	tr
Oatmeal, cooked	1 cup	5	23	2	—
Rice, raw:					
Brown	1 cup	15	154	3	—
White, enriched	1 cup	12	149	1	—
Rye wafers	2	2	10	tr	—
Wheat flakes, enriched	1 cup	3	24	tr	—
Wheat germ	1 cup	17	34	7	3
SWEETS					
Honey, strained	1 tb.	tr	17	0	—
Molasses:					
Blackstrap	1 tb.	—	11	—	—
Light	1 tb.	—	13	—	—
Sugar, brown	1 cup	0	212	0	—
NUTS AND SEEDS					
Almonds	1 cup	26	28	77	6
Cashews	1 cup	24	41	64	11
Coconut, shredded	1 cup	5	12	46	39
Peanut butter	1 tb.	4	3	8	2
Peanuts, roasted	1 cup	37	27	72	16
Sesame seeds	1 cup	18	20	48	26
Sunflower seeds	1 cup	24	20	52	14
Walnuts, English chopped	1 cup	14	16	64	14
NUTRITIONAL SUPPLEMENTS					
Bone meal or powder	1 tsp.	0	0	0	0
Calcium gluconate	7½ tsp.	0	0	0	0
Calcium lactate	3½ tsp.	0	0	0	0
Dicalcium phosphate	1 tsp.	0	0	0	0
Lecithin, granular	2 tb.	0	0	11	9
Liver, dessicated, defatted	¼ cup	28	3	tr	—
Yeast, brewer's, debittered	¼ cup	13	12	tr	tr

Lino-leic acid grams	Calcium mg.	Iron mg.	Vitamins				
			A units	B₁ mg.	B₂ mg.	Niacin mg.	C mg.
—	2	.7	150	.10	.07	1.0	0
2	24	2.9	620	.46	.13	2.4	0
—	147	.7	0	.12	.07	1.0	0
11	218	8.8	121	.9	.3	2.3	0
—	18	3.3	0	.51	.30	4.0	0
1	49	4.0	0	.66	.14	5.2	0
1	22	1.4	0	.19	.05	.2	0
—	78	4	0	.6	.1	9.2	0
—	44	5.4	0	.81	.06	6.5	0
—	7	.5	0	.04	.03	.2	0
—	12	1.3	0	.19	.04	1.5	0
3	57	5.5	0	1.4	.5	3.1	0
—	1	.1	0	tr	.01	.1	tr
—	137	3.2	—	.02	.04	.4	—
—	33	.9	—	.01	.01	tr	—
—	187	7.5	0	.02	.07	.4	0
15	332	6.7	0	.34	1.31	5.0	tr
4	53	5.3	140	.60	.35	2.5	—
tr	17	2.2	0	.07	.03	.7	4
2	9	.3	—	.02	.02	2.4	0
21	107	3.0	—	.46	.19	24.7	0
20	1,160	10.4	30	.8	.2	5.4	0
30	120	7.0	0	3.6	.4	27.2	0
40	100	3.0	30	.2	.2	.8	2
0	2,000	3.6	0	0	0	0	0
0	1,000	0	0	0	0	0	0
0	1,000	0	0	0	0	0	0
0	1,000	0	0	0	0	0	0
2.4	tr	tr	—	—	—	—	—
—	20	12	0	.2	4.4	11.3	70
tr	70	5	tr	5.2	1	12.9	0

tr = trace   — = lack of reliable data

index

310